"BLOODY DECKS AND A BUMPER CROP": THE RHETORIC OF SEALING COUNTER-PROTEST

Cynthia Lamson

Social and Economic Studies No. 24
Institute of Social and Economic Research
Memorial University of Newfoundland
St. John's, Newfoundland
1979

TABLE OF CONTENTS

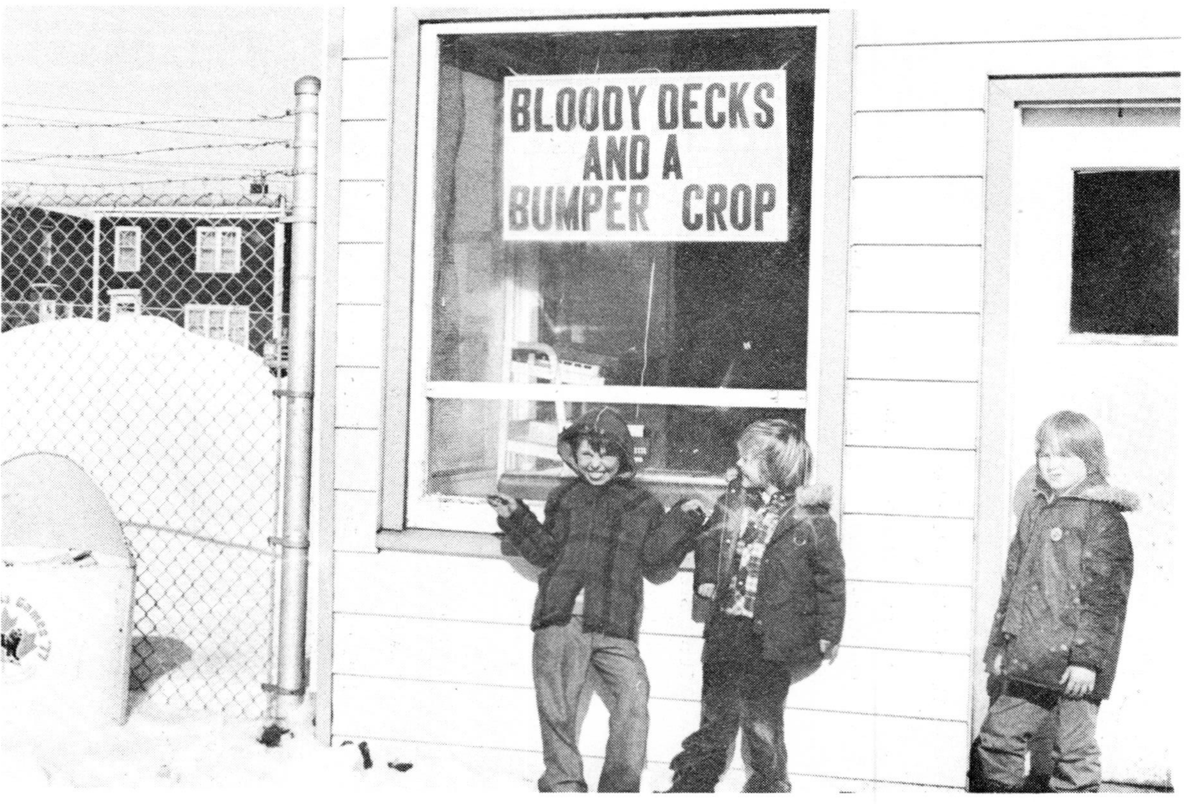
BLOODY DECKS
AND A
BUMPER CROP

ACKNOWLEDGEMENTS

I would like to thank Dean Frederick A. Aldrich who made my studies at Memorial University possible through generous fellowship support. To my graduate supervisor, Dr. Kenneth S. Goldstein, I would like to express my gratitude for his guidance and continuing faith in my work. I am indebted to Dr. Robert Paine for sharing his thoughts about rhetoric with me, and to the Institute of Social and Economic Research for their support in seeing this book through to publication.

Fellow students in the Folklore Department deserve much credit for their sustained enthusiasm, and I appreciate their almost daily words of encouragement. To the poets of Newfoundland and, in particular, those verse-makers who consented to assist me with this work, I owe a thank-you which cannot be adequately expressed. I can only say that my gratitude comes from the heart.

Sonia Paine was an instructive editor, and Jeanette Gleeson was patient and cheerful despite the problems presented by transforming a messy typescript into a legible manuscript.

Finally, I would like to dedicate this book to two very special Newfoundlanders whose friendship I will always cherish--Marilyn Gould and Marilyn Willcott.

NOTE

Chapter notes appear at the end of the text, and complete references are provided on pages 101-103. An asterisk appears where occasional explanatory notes were necessary, and the information is given at the bottom of the appropriate page. Quotations and verses have been reprinted exactly as collected, therefore errors in spelling and punctuation may occur throughout the text.

The frontispiece photograph was taken by the author in March, 1978, at Hugh Shea's grocery store on Field Street, St. John's. The three final pages of the book contain (1) a sketch reproduced from the St. John's Jaycee publication, "Facts About the Seal Harvest," (1978); (2) the logo from the Greenpeace 1978 press release brochure, and (3) the countering logo of the 1979 Codpeace campaign.

PREFACE

The spring seal hunt in Newfoundland has been a traditional activity for centuries. It has been the source and inspiration for innumerable songs, stories and anecdotes, which provide Newfoundlanders with a distinctive heritage. The title of this book is, in fact, a celebrated sealers' toast.

The last decade has witnessed a curious phenomenon--sealing has been challenged by outsiders on social, moral and ethical grounds. The campaign intensified from its initial whisperings in the late 1950s to a full-scale, international issue by the mid-'60s. As the protest became institutionalized with formal organizations and leadership, Newfoundlanders were forced to respond, not only to protect their industry but, more importantly, to defend their pride and cultural identity. This is a study of their counter-protest. Whereas protest implies criticism or opposition, counter-protest rationalizes and defends the _status quo_. Counter-protest can take a variety of forms, and to the extent that I have tried to delineate these forms, this work is descriptive. More importantly, I have attempted to identify certain rhetorical strategies that seem to be central to the pro-sealing cause.

Searching through back issues of the St. John's _Evening Telegram_, I discovered several poems about the sealing controversy. At the same time, the Provincial Government was conducting an international campaign to defend the annual hunt and local newspapers were reporting and editorializing about the anticipated protest in March, 1978. Having read Cassie Brown's _Death on the Ice_ at Christmas, and being absolutely spellbound by that account, I was emotionally geared to listen to all new reports about current sealing practices.

As a student of folklore, I thought it might be instructive to compare contemporary verses with traditional sealing songs. In the process of collecting material, I came to the realization that protest and counter-protest were themes that transcended formal, generic boundaries--that the actual form of the expression is secondary to message and delivery. With this in mind, I expanded my research effort to the broader topic of counter-protest, considering any material that met the following conditions: (1) the item expressed an opinion about the protest or protesters, and (2) this opinion was shared with others and therefore was a deliberate communicative act rather than a personal, idiosyncratic and introspective act.

Counter-movements are a recurring phenomena but few have been seriously studied by social scientists.[1] Part of the difficulty is that each conflict has certain novel, time-specific dimensions. Perhaps the principal benefit of a study of counter-movements is that it provides information about a culture which is otherwise inaccessible or speculative.

Cultural groups may have certain ideas about their own identity, as contrasted with other groups, but they are not always verbalized.[2] Conflict situations generate a heightened sense of self-consciousness; esoteric and exoteric attitudes come to the surface and often form the core of expressive counter-protest. Through a diachronic analysis of repeated thematic responses, we are able to identify traditional values as well as document the emergence of a culturally-based rhetoric.

To articulate the features of the sealing counter-protest in Newfoundland, I have selected examples from popular communication channels: letters-to-the-editor, open-line radio programs, books, magazines, and the like. Some items were referrals from friends and associates who were kind enough to share my interest and their knowledge, but I cannot ignore my debt to the serendipity factor. In February, 1978, I submitted a brief letter to the editors of provincial newspapers requesting contemporary sealing verses. Chapter three contains the material collected, and though I can hardly claim it to be complete, I do feel confident that it is representative of current sentiment and expressive strategy.

It is my sincere hope that through this study, a small but significant part of Newfoundland's social history will have been recorded. It remains to be seen how long the anti-sealing campaign continues, but it is certain Newfoundlanders will not readily forget this era of provocation and conflict.

CHAPTER I

THE SEALING CONTROVERSY

International public interest in sealing began in the late 1950s. The protest and counter-protest movements of the '70s were preceded by vigorous debate between humane societies and the Federal Government while the sealers themselves remained silent.

A partial explanation of the indignation and defensive attitude taken by Newfoundlanders today lies in the fact that abusive sealing practices cited in the '60s were rectified through strict government regulation. Continuous supervision by the Department of Fisheries now insures that sealing quotas are respected and that killing is conducted by humane methods.

One essential fact is often neglected in public accounts of the situation--the protest originated with observations of sealing activities in the Magdalen Islands where two separate groups were involved: landsmen from the Magdalens and sealers from Newfoundland vessels. Criticism was directed at the landsmen who were largely inexperienced and unsupervised. In contrast, the ship-based sealers were observed to be disciplined, orderly and responsible to experienced captains who would not condone abuses.[1] Ice conditions during recent years have made sealing difficult in the Magdalens, and so the focus of world attention has shifted to the Newfoundland hunt. Unfortunately, films of Magdalen abuses are still circulated to stir up public opinion, and too few people are aware of the critical distinctions between the two operations.

PROTEST, PROTESTERS AND IDEOLOGY

Since my primary interest is with the response of Newfoundlanders, the narrative begins in 1976[2] with the first confrontation between "come-from-away"* protesters and sealers, when Brian Davies hired a team of airline stewardesses to accompany himself and a crew of reporters to the ice. Sealers were instructed to ignore the protesters who shouted, "You butchers, you bloody butchers. Do you sleep at night . . . will you be able to eat your dinner today? You must feel very brave killing those little animals. What men, what brave men."[3] Davies was later charged with two violations of the Seal

---

*"Come-from-away" is a Newfoundland expression for anyone born outside the province.

Protection Regulations: for landing a helicopter less than one-half nautical mile from any seal, and operating a chopper over seals at an altitude of less than 2,000 feet.[4]

After a public meeting with St. Anthony residents and other concerned citizens, the Greenpeace Foundation agreed not to spray-paint the seals, but they maintained their avowed position to see the whitecoat hunt abolished. Junior Abbott, a Musgrave Harbour man, gave this interpretation of the 1976 protesters:

> I'll give my opinion on the female people who are going to come down here. We all have long hair and modern looks. What are they supposed to be, the Delilah of the new age? And what are they going to do, cut off our hair and poke our eyes out? I had my wife with me last year; she was out for a week with me and nobody knew she was a woman from the way she dressed. So I can only picture these young ladies out there in sheer cloth and those poor things are going to freeze to death.[5]

There were no incidents at the ice, but there were many threats in anticipation of aggravation. "Newfoundland people are like the Newfoundland dog who is very kind and very gentle until you make him angry and then he can become very vicious."[6] Senator F. W. Rowe was sufficiently concerned before the opening of the hunt to send a letter of warning to Romeo LeBlanc, Federal Fisheries Minister:

> We must be realistic in this matter and recognize that seal hunters are armed with lethal instruments . . . it would require only one sealer out of hundreds involved, to be goaded to the point of desperation, for a tragedy to result . . .; Moreover, the possibility of a fatal accident should not be overlooked, especially if, as reported in today's <u>Globe and Mail</u>, Mr. Brian Davies carries out the unbelievably stupid suggestion of using airline stewardesses to interfere with the seal hunt.[7]

The 1977 protest in St. Anthony was a carnival with a number of side-shows. Brian Davies rented the entire Viking Motel for his contingent of press and protesters. On March 14, an estimated crowd of 250 to 300 demonstrators surrounded Davies' helicopters, and others tried to delay his departure by blocking the motel exit with their bodies. Nearly a hundred RCMP officers were called in to protect Davies and ensure that there would be no violence.

The failure of both the Federal and Provincial Governments to take a firm stand on behalf of the sealing industry led, in 1978, to the formation of two independent counter-protest organizations, the Concerned Citizens of St. Anthony and the Trinity Bay Society for the Retention of Our Sealing Industry, and it was the combined membership of these two groups that manned the picket lines that spring. Provincial Fisheries Minister, Walter Carter, made himself unpopular by warning the demonstrators not to engage in any illegal activity, with the result that many viewed him as a political sellout. After a 24-hour vigil at the Viking Motel, a public meeting was convened at the St. Anthony High School auditorium and attended by some 400 people. Carter, local politicians, fisheries officers, and representatives of the clergy stood together on the platform to tell the audience, "We're fighting for our very survival in Newfoundland," and warned, "Protesters should not interpret our patience as weakness."[8]

The protest contingent featured two movie stars, Yvette Mimieux and Brigette Bardot, creating a minor distraction for the press. But they did not accomplish much in the way of obstructing the hunt. Bardot apparently appeared at the invitation of Franz Weber, a Swiss millionaire-conservationist, who joined the ranks of protesters in 1977. At a February news conference in St. John's, Weber announced his plans to establish a synthetic fur industry to recompense the Newfoundland sealers once the hunt was abolished. He also revealed that his offer "to buy" the lives of baby seals for $400,000 had been rejected by Romeo LeBlanc. Weber's plans to charter a "floating hotel" to accommodate 600 journalists to witness the hunt were greeted with amusement by the local press and public.

The Greenpeace Foundation set up their headquarters in Blanc Sablon, Quebec, across the Strait of Belle Isle. The rationale for staying at a distance was articulated by Patrick Moore: "They'd love to turn this into a Greenpeace _versus_ Newfoundlanders thing, rather than Greenpeacers _versus_ the seal hunt thing. That's why we're not getting involved in any of the demonstrations. We're not accusing the people here of anything."[9] One of the Greenpeace team gained notoriety for hand-cuffing himself to the hauling winches of the "Martin Karlsen" as the seal pelts were being loaded. Paul Watson was dunked several times in the ocean, but was later taken aboard and given dry clothes and food. Greenpeace press releases suggested the dunking was deliberate, but other reporters on the scene did not concur.

One of the most distressing aspects of the protest was the receipt of hate letters addressed to St. Anthony residents. Many of them were written by elementary school children and were filled with vicious threats. The

St. Anthony Concerned Citizens' Committee returned bundles of the mail to United States Senator, Edward Kennedy, and President Jimmy Carter, suggesting that schools were inappropriate places for propaganda.

On 22 March, 1977, the United States House of Representatives heard a resolution, introduced by Congressman Leo Ryan (California), which called on the "Canadian government to review its policy of allowing the 'barbarous' killing of new-born seals in the annual hunt; . . . . killing seals by clubbing them on the head is a cruel practice that may cause the species to become extinct." The Canadian House of Commons responded on 24 March with a resolution of support for the annual hunt, stating all efforts would be made to ensure strict supervision.[10]

As previously noted, two independent citizens' groups had been formed to counter the protest since official government policy was to ignore the protesters. However, in 1977, the Newfoundland government contributed $6,000 to the organizations in support of their efforts. In May, the St. Anthony Concerned Citizens merged with the Trinity Bay Society for the Retention of the Sealing Industry, and they drew up a constitution for the new body, the Progressive Rights Organization (PRO). Article 2 contains their statement of purpose: "To inform people of their rights, to act as an agency to insure these rights are respected and upheld to the end, that they may be able to effectively counter misinformation and propaganda in respect to the way of life in the Province of Newfoundland and Labrador . . ."

In 1978, the Progressive Rights Organization was funded by a Canada Works grant, by the Resource Foundation for the Arts, and the Provincial Government. Eight people were hired to work for the twenty-week period corresponding to the annual protest effort. Their duties included answering letters of inquiry from outside the province, as well as soliciting support from industry and service organizations within the province.

The PRO revived the traditional sealers' send-off ceremony and on 5 March, 1978, an estimated crowd of 4,000 well-wishers attended the waterfront service conducted by representatives from all the major religious denominations in St. John's. In St. Anthony, PRO headquarters were open to the public, where members were available to answer questions and provide information about the hunt.

Premier Frank Moores and the Newfoundland Government finally took an aggressive stand *vis-à-vis* the protesters in early 1978. A series of press conferences in New York, Boston, Washington, Chicago, Toronto, Montreal,

Ottawa, San Francisco, Los Angeles, Vancouver, Winnipeg, Paris, London, and Frankfurt were scheduled to present the Newfoundland position on the hunt. Essentially a media campaign, it was directed at journalists who heretofore had been exposed to the protesters' arguments only. Moores was accompanied by Walter Carter, Provincial Fisheries Minister; John Lundrigan, the Minister of Industrial and Rural Development; Thomas Jughes, Executive Vice-President of the Ontario Humane Society; Dr. Joseph MacInnis, marine biologist; Dr. Harry Rowsell and Dr. H. Bruno Schiefer, pathologists; Mac Mercer, senior policy advisor with the Department of Fisheries; Jim Winter, a CBC commentator; and Captain Morrissey Johnson, skipper of the Newfoundland vessel, the "Lady Johnson II."

The protest itself was quiet in comparison to those held in 1976 and 1977. Only Greenpeace returned to Newfoundland, but Brian Davies remained vocal in his efforts to arouse sympathy for his cause in Europe. On 27 February, 1978, Greenpeace members, in rubber rafts, attempted to obstruct the sealing vessels as they left the Halifax harbour en route to St. John's. Though law enforcement agencies were prepared for a repeat attempt in St. John's on 5 March, there were no further incidents.

Twenty Greenpeacers made the trip to St. Anthony, including two screen actresses and two United States congressmen, James Jeffords (Vermont) and Leo Ryan (California). Newfoundlanders were angered by the presence of the Congressmen, and John Lundrigan confronted them at the ice, saying, "Go back and straighten up your own country and get your own house in order."[11] It was never clear why the two were in St. Anthony, although Mr. Jeffords stated he was there at the invitation of the Canadian Government.[12]

In 1978, Greenpeace activity was hampered both by ice conditions and new Fisheries Department regulations. The seals were whelping off the coast of Labrador, making them inaccessible to helicopters from St. Anthony; in addition, permits were mandatory for anyone wishing to observe the hunt (Appendix 2), and anyone whose express purpose was to obstruct the hunt was denied a permit. Dr. Patrick Moore was arrested on two occasions: once for trepassing when he refused to leave a temporary Department of Fisheries office at the St. Anthony motel, and later, for sitting on a seal to protect it from being clubbed (the charge was for obstructing the hunt). The possibility for further activity was aborted when the Fisheries Department announced that the press would not be allowed to accompany a Greenpeace member to the scene of sealing operations, in effect, eliminating all opportunities for publicity.

In order to understand why an anti-sealing campaign occurred at all, it is necessary to consider the issue in the larger context of the environmental movement. "Earth Day," 22 April, 1970, is the acknowledged birthdate of the contemporary environmental movement. ". . . now, more than ever before, nature appears to have acquired expressive meaning for the American people rather than being, as before, merely an object for consumptive use and conquest."[13] A legacy of earlier preservation and conservation interests, ". . . this movement must be viewed as one of the most important social movements of recent history. It evolved out of a growing belief that the world faces an ultimate 'eco-catastrophe' unless immediate and successful efforts are made to halt the destruction of the environment, and has gone on to attract the support of hundreds of thousands of people in its cause."[14] The activists are drawn from an educated elite, with access to wealth and the coercive means to affect protest and, ultimately, change.[15] For example, sealing protester, Pamela Sue Martin, commented to a CBC reporter:

> . . . it's a shame to treat nature this way in this day and age, because with the seals, there are substitutes for anything they can possibly get from the seals . . . I'm constantly impressed with the beauty here and the way everything is, . . . I would think the people here would want to preserve their resources and preserve this area and keep it this way always.[16]

Newfoundlanders, on the other hand, do not perceive the protest in light of environmental degradation, but as a direct threat to their traditional way of life and economic welfare. Since this point will be argued in greater detail in the following chapters, I will not elaborate here except to suggest that the two sides will never be in agreement while social and economic discrepancies remain between them.

COUNTER-PROTEST: THEME AND EXPRESSIONS

Counter-protest is reactionary (counter-actionary), usually defensive and often aggressive in tone. Sometimes it strives to persuade, but its essential functions are to justify and rationalize. Highly suggestible, it seizes upon themes, characters and events that emerge from protest situations. It is conservative rather than innovative in that it responds to, and elaborates upon, situations already created by protesters.

When Newfoundlanders realized the sealing protest was no longer an irritating amusement, but a threat to the future of the hunt, defiant voices of counter-protest began to be raised. Government or "official" counter-protest was directed to audiences on the Canadian mainland, in

Europe, and the United States. Statistics and scientific data were presented at press conferences and distributed in brochures to document economic need and to counter charges of cruelty and species depletion.

In contrast, individuals were not compelled or constrained to respond with cool reason, and many Newfoundlanders were openly angry. Their expressions were typically emotional, and they utilized a variety of channels to communicate them. Although the intended audience was external, it was also largely inaccessible, and so the majority of counter-protesters were addressing members of their own interest group. Rather than reverse critical opinions, counter-protest functioned to affirm allegiance and renew a cultural self-consciousness.

Visual Statements

A number of visual statements supporting the seal hunt appeared as counter-protest expressions. The bumper-sticker with the motto: "S.O.S. Save Our Swilers," is a notable combination because there is the underlying implication that it is the sealers ("swilers") and not the harp seals that are endangered. The pronoun, "our," implicates the entire province; whereas only a few hundred men engage in the ship-based hunt each year, the conflict is perceived as a threat to all Newfoundlanders. In Corner Brook, the annual snow-sculpture contest inspired Wayne Hartson to make a political statement: "Leave Our Newfoundland Seal Hunters Alone." The sculpture, depicting a sealer and whitecoat pup, was transformed from a familiar cultural figure into a symbolic counter-protest message. In another example, the owner of a St. John's grocery used his front window to demonstrate support for sealers in March, 1978. "Bloody Decks and a Bumper Crop," is a traditional toast which was restored to public consciousness primarily through media repetition. Hugh Shea's sign was an extremely esoteric form of counter-protest, for the message is interpretable only to those familiar with the folk expression.

Other visual statements of counter-protest included buttons, comic strips and cartoons. Several cartoons by Joe Connolly[17] are included in Chapter 2 of this book to illustrate common rhetorical arguments.

Electronic Media

Radio played a vital role in stimulating counter-protest. By continuous news coverage, ranging from advance speculation about protest activities, to editorials, and on-the-spot reporting, the controversy was very much in the public domain. Martin Hurley, a disc jockey for the Corner Brook CF station, sponsored a "PPP" campaign during the first week of the whitecoat hunt in 1978.

"Protesters Protesting Protesters" inspired some 4,000 calls from listeners in the Humber Valley and the Northern Peninsula. Hurley summarized the majority opinion: "most were disgusted our hunters had to put up with so much bull and so many uneducated people interfering in a man's right to make a living at something that does not destroy the elements or upset the balance of nature."[18] The PPP had its own theme song, composed and recorded by Reg Watkins,[19] who was appointed honorary chairman of the group. The phrase, "uneducated people," occurs repeatedly in counter-protest expressions, and yet is somewhat ironic considering the above-average educational level of most environmental activists. The reference is intended to connote ignorance about the seal fishery and the Newfoundland economy, and to discredit those who make malicious and inflammatory charges about Newfoundlanders.

When the former sealer-turned-protester, Ray Elliott, returned to St. John's after appearing at European press conferences with Brian Davies, a three-way phone hook-up was arranged on open-line radio shows so that callers could address Elliott, the moderator, or both. Newfoundlanders were embittered and angry that one of their own could make false statements about sealing, and be quoted by the international press as an authority. Whereas many callers disputed Elliott's claim about skinning pups alive, the majority used the opportunity to pour abuse on Elliott's character and denounce his "betrayal." Typical of the remarks made on the morning of 27 February, 1978 were as follows:

> Caller: "You know you're just like Judas Iscariot, he sold Jesus for 30 pieces of silver, and you're selling Newfoundlanders for a trip over to Europe."
>
> Caller: "You know . . . there should be someone there to tar you and feather you and burn ya . . . cause you're lower than an eel in a bucket of snot . . . if I was as low as you, I'd cut me throat . . . you're only sick, you're dirt, scum . . ."
>
> Caller: "Traitor, I hope you choke on a nice juicy steak from a nice brown-eyed cow, or are you waiting for spring, for a nice little lamb?"
>
> Caller: "Carl, I wish you'd get this man off the air; he's the devil himself . . ."[20]

Many callers threatened Elliott with bodily harm in retaliation for his disloyalty, but the confrontations never materialized. Though it is impossible to measure Elliott's role in activating the counter-protest in

1978, his short-lived notoriety was certainly instrumental in arousing heated sentiment among Newfoundlanders. Elliott may have given Davies' cause extra vigour in Europe, but his controversial stand also renewed interest at home. The open-line programs simply picked up on a news item, and the listening audience seized the opportunity to counter-attack. With the assistance of provocative comments by radio moderators, Elliott quickly became synonymous with Judas Iscariot in the public mind.

Dramatization

An account of the controversy would be incomplete without reference to several other events, notably the activities planned by the PRO, and the Mummer's Play, "They Club Seals, Don't They?" The troupe toured across Canada during the spring of 1978 and appeared in St. Anthony on the eve of the official opening of the seal hunt. The local auditorium was filled to capacity by local citizens and journalists, and reaction to the creative re-enactment of the controversy and its attendant issues was extremely favourable.

The PRO hired a staff of writers to answer letters of inquiry, to solicit moral and financial support from service organizations and private business, and to plan activities which would focus positive attention on the seal hunt during the month of March, 1978. In St. John's, the sending-off ceremony--a tradition which had lapsed for thirty years--was attended by an estimated crowd of 4,000 people. Brief speeches by officials and sealing captains were followed by prayers offered by representatives of the clergy. The departing fleet was saluted by church bells and ships' horns in a loud and demonstrative display of support.

The spirit of public camaraderie carried well into the night of 5 March, as local pubs were jammed with crowds of exuberant well-wishers. At the Rob Roy pub, the music group "Home Brew," improvised an appropriate verse to their rendition of the "Drunken Sailor" song. In reply to the question, "What do you do with Brian Davies, what do you do with Brian Davies . . .," the musical answer was given: "Shave his balls with a rusty razor." The crowd shouted approval, and the group retained the verse for the following fortnight at regular club appearances.

In St. Anthony, PRO headquarters were open to the public. A display of work by the Newfoundland artist, David Blackwood, at the local Lions' Club and a traditional crafts' exhibit were further efforts to demonstrate to protesters and visiting journalists that Newfoundlanders have a creative, aesthetic dimension.

Publications

A book of traditional sealing songs and poetry, Haulin' Rope and Gaff, was released by Breakwater Books, Ltd., in March, 1978. The publisher suggested one rationale for reproducing folk material in such an elaborate format was partially to refute the charge that sealers are barbarians. In effect, the message was simply that sealers have the capacity to be poets as well as harvesters of the sea.[21]

Two service organizations, the Newfoundland and Labrador Women's Institute and the St. John's Jaycees, adopted resolutions to support the seal hunt. Both accepted responsibility for providing facts to affiliate groups throughout Canada in an effort to reach people with alternative information.

> (Resolved) . . . that we urge the Provincial Government to mount counter-advertising to show the true picture of the Hunt, to provide protection to the sealers by introducing a law prohibiting non-sealers from going to the ice, and that Newfoundland and Labrador Women's Institutes do all it [sic] can to pass on the true information of our Sealing Industry through Federated Women's Institutes of Canada (F.W.I.C.) and associated Country Women of the World (A.C.W.W.).[22]

The Jaycee publication included this message: "This document is dedicated to the truth and is being distributed by the St. John's Jaycee Unit to help combat, 'the big lie.'"[23] In contrast to the official seal-hunt brochure printed by the Department of Fisheries and Environment, the Jaycees' message was more defensive and provocative. Inclusion of a sketch depicting a seal with a pig face and the caption, "Let's be honest, it really does make a difference," (p. 109), is an obvious example of appeal through emotion as well as intellect.

Finally, a special issue of Decks Awash, a bi-monthly publication of the Memorial University Extension Service, was devoted to the seal hunt. The introduction states the editorial position: ". . . the controversy has gone far beyond the rational, scientific, and humane levels and entered into the realm of hysterical emotionalism. Unfortunately, those who are bearing the brunt of this mass hysteria are Newfoundlanders, and yet the hunt involves many more people who refuse to look in their own backyards."[24] An effort to examine objectively all aspects of the seal hunt, the publication specifically addressed issues raised by critics, and justification was argued via personal experience narratives--rather than bluntly asserting the right of Newfoundlanders to pursue the hunt.

THE COUNTER-PROTEST ARGUMENT

To the urbanite ecologists, the seal hunt issue is fundamentally a scientific and philosophical problem. In contrast, Newfoundlanders interpret the dispute as a challenge to their traditional independence and livelihood. Richard Cashin, in a much applauded speech, made this observation: "The issue of the seal hunt is theological and we are experiencing a new paganism. We are substituting sentiment for faith and we worship an adorable little seal or some other fetish or symbol. In fact, Greenpeace, Brian Davies, and many supposedly intelligent and prominent people in the Western world have given the seal a soul."[25]

Initially, anti-hunt agitation was confusing--even incomprehensible--to Newfoundlanders but, through time, categories of accusations could be identified and patterned counter-arguments were articulated. In order of the frequency with which they were cited, these may be classified as: (1) economic necessity, (2) tradition, (3) occupational hazard, (4) ecological responsibility, and (5) divine sanction. Whereas the government campaign sought to contradict the protesters' charges with authoritative evidence, counter-protest by individuals relied on testimonials (eye-witness accounts and personal reminiscences). The essential points of each counter-argument are presented in the following pages.

(1) Economic Necessity

> I wonder if Brian Davies or his co-workers ever heard a child cry for a slice of bread and molasses. Many of those families had a very limited amount of food in the home until their fathers returned from the ice floes.[26]

The economic value of the hunt is perhaps the most disputed issue of the entire controversy. Whereas protesters argue that the number of Newfoundlanders who actually benefit financially from the hunt is limited (approximately 4,000), the Provincial Government utilizes the same figure to demonstrate how the entire Atlantic economy is bolstered during an otherwise restricted season.[27] Benefits fluctuate considerably from year to year, but landsmen frequently suggest that they derive as much as a third of their total income from sealing: "I start sealing about April 1 and I get about one-third of my income from that. Then, at the last of May to the middle of June, I start at the salmon fishery, from which I get another third of my income. After a month or so at that, I start at the cod fishery, which gives me the other third. All in all, the three lots combined give me my livelihood. To cut off that is going to hurt me."[28]

In terms of popular opinion, statistics carry little weight. The fact that so many people believe the seal hunt is crucial to the province's economy is the relevant point. To quote a sealer about to depart for the ice in 1976: ". . . if they're out there trying to stop a man from making a living, there's going to be trouble."[29]

(2) Tradition

> To the Newfoundland sealer, the seal hunt was part of his livelihood, an industry passed on to him by his father, his grandfather, and his great grandfather, and he sought to perpetuate it with dignity and pride.[30]

> . . . it is part of our heritage, our soul and also our need to work for our bread instead of taking hand-outs.[31]

Seal-hunt opponents dismiss the 'tradition' argument, saying it is unfortunate but nonetheless ecologically necessary to abolish the hunt. They fail to recognize that sealing is not a single, isolated activity affecting only a small number of individuals. Even the official brochure makes this point: ". . . dollars and cents do not tell a full story. Sealing is an enterprise with an air of adventure, pursued in a hostile environment which tests the mettle of its participants. It is part of a cultural heritage.[32]

Sealing was an adventure with an economic incentive. The opportunity for outport men to go to the ice at a time of the year when other activities were restricted was greatly anticipated. Traditionally, men who participated in the hunt enjoyed increased prestige in their home communities for several reasons: (1) often a man's credit rating with the local merchant was increased;[33] (2) in an otherwise cashless economy, the hunt gave participants cash to buy items they otherwise could not afford;[34] and finally, (3) exciting esoteric experiences were the source of entertainment (and instruction) among family members of a sealer and in larger social gatherings. According to Scott's study of the function of folklore at the seal fishery ". . . it is the function of folklore to give men this ability to cope with conditions and dangers of the seal fishery. Also folklore functions to increase the rewards for participation in the hunt by allowing those people outside the occupation to hold an overly dramatic picture of the hazards of sealing."[35]

The second point is repeated in the familiar verse:

> Harbour Grace is a pretty place
> And so is Peeley's Island
> Daddy's going to buy me a brand new dress
> When the boys come home from swilin'.[36]

Sealing stories were integral features of community lore. Hardship, disasters, humorous incidents, and great sealing successes were subject to repetition, often inspiring the composition of songs and verses. The anthology, Haulin' Rope and Gaff, is testimony to the range of topics and attitudes towards the seal fishery. The oldest recorded song dates from 1833, and the fact that sealing songs are still being composed at the present time reflects an enduring fascination with the subject.

Family stories were the source of pride and awe. Bella Hodge's is a good example:

> One time, I remember my father went to Lance aux Meadows on dog team with five others. One man died and my father was found covered in snow with just his hands sticking up. One man reached home and told how the men were lost and a rescue team went for them. Then they brought my father home. He was frozen just like a chunk of ice. It took all night for my grandmother and the other women to bring him to.[37]

Such stories help formulate popular opinion about the fishery; yet there is a vague recognition that they may not be completely accurate. As one veteran sealer told an interviewer: "He (McKay) is very glad that he went and nowadays when he hears people talking about the Front and what goes on, or what they think goes on, he does not have to rely on what they are saying because he has been there himself and he knows for himself what happens at the Front."[38]

(3) Occupational Hazard

> These fishermen, in their efforts to provide the necessities of life for their families, are engaged in an occupation noted for its hardship and hazard. They will not take kindly to the efforts of misguided zealots who threaten to interfere with their lawful activities.[39]

Occupational hazard is an argument voiced by non-sealers, though references are frequently made to past experiences of friends or relatives. With technological advances and a less-competitive attitude towards sealing, the degree of physical danger has decreased considerably. Although there are always uncertain perils at sea or on the ice, it is now chiefly the recollection of hardship and tragedy that survives in the folk memory.

> Many of these brave men died at sea, not from poor health, but through great battles with the very unpredictable Atlantic ice fields. A neighbour once told me that he saw brave men grow weak and became foolish when they discovered that the strong winds and currents had separated them from their ship, some men wandered away and were never seen again, and others just gave up hope and froze to death. Some bodies were saved, but others were claimed by the sea, it has a demand too, for human life.[40]

> Tell me, Miss Bardot, do you recall at lamplight melting ice with your breath from the kitchen window? Yes, ten tiny faces peeping through, looking, waiting anxiously for a dad long overdue from the seal hunt, risking his life (for you) hopping from pan of ice to pan of ice in deathly chilling waters for barely enough money to buy molasses and tea.[41]

Scott suggests that: ". . . the esoteric picture of the hazards is certainly darker than that which is held by the sealers themselves. If the people at home wanted to see the hunt as fraught with perils, the sealers were in no hurry to correct them."[42] The risk of losing a chance to supplement their income was, to the sealers, more threatening than physical danger.

(4) Ecological Responsibility

The stability of the harp seal population has been debated by biologists, government officials, environmentalists, sealers, and the public. Unfortunately, since harp seals whelp on floating ice, it is impossible to determine the species' population with complete accuracy. Various measurement methods have produced contradictory results and, therefore, opposing groups are at liberty to select data which corroborates their position.

In a rather heated television interview with Dan MacDermott, a Greenpeace member of the 1978 Halifax harbour exploit, Rex Murphy elicited the following:

> Murphy: One of your people said today at your press conference that you were obeying higher laws than the laws of the land. It suggests to me that you've got special rights or some special qualifications to interpret the higher laws, that you set yourselves above people . . . where is your connection with this higher set

of laws than those the rest of us are supposed to live by?

MacDermott: We maintain that the most important thing for people on the face of the earth is to keep the earth a viable ecosystem. We maintain that wiping out a species, such as the harp seal, is an extreme circumstance which calls for extreme measures to make sure that stops. Many prominent scientists, not just Dr. David Lavigne, feel that it is ecologically insane to commercially exploit a species that is below its maximum sustainable yield.[43]

Interestingly, the harp seal does not appear on any official endangered species list and, according to Fisheries Department biologist, Mac Mercer, the harp is the second most populous species of the planet's thirty-two types of seal. Even Dr. David Lavigne denied the alarmist position taken by protesters at a conference in March, 1978 in St. John's.[44]

The two most familiar testimonials of counter-protest are: (1) assurances about the increasing size of the seal herds, and (2) the concomitant depletion of capelin stocks.

> A ban on sealing, for example, could produce disastrous changes in the capelin stock, as capelin form a large part of the diet of the Harp seal. What's 'good' for the seal could ruin the capelin stocks, which would in turn have a detrimental effect on stocks of another fish, such as cod, which feed upon capelin. It's like a chain on a highway.[45]

The St. Anthony Polaris News conducted an interview with a local fisherman and inquired about the relationship between seals and the abundance of cod:

> . . . our cod fish is in worse danger than the seals . . . any fisherman can tell you they are watching the fishery going down from the past three years; if one million seals ate one pound of fish a day, multiply that by 365 and you've got 365 million. If you let those seals multiply you got one million this year, in two years' time, you'd have two million.[46]

What angers Newfoundlanders is the apparent assumption by protesters that they are unconcerned with natural laws. To quote Cliff Reardon again, "if they could point out to me that the seals are in danger, I'd be the first one to say yes, ban the hunt."[47] Thus, by 1978, the typical countering argument acknowledges the changing Greenpeace emphasis on ecosystems: "it is common sense that if we harvest a percentage of the prey (fish), then we must also harvest a percentage of the predator (seal) if we are to maintain nature's delicate balance.[48]

(5) Divine Sanction

> God put seals in the world like he did every other animal for the use of man. It is mentioned in the Good Book. Therefore killing them is no different from killing all the other animals we eat.[49]

Occasionally, divine ordinance is cited as justification for the pursuit of seals. A more common practice is to invoke God's blessing for a safe voyage. Traditionally, seals were not killed on Sundays, and often church services were held aboard ship. As a demonstration of community support and thanksgiving, church bells were rung when ships departed and again when they returned.

> I felt very proud for Newfoundlanders when I heard they were going to send their great heroes off to the 1978 hunt in prayers, prayers for a prosperous hunt and a safe return to 'Home Sweet Home.' I would have enjoyed this event because when I was young the church bells used to ring out to sealers returning home from the hunt. I can recall a wonderful aunt of mine lighting the latern and placing it in a light tower near the shoreline to direct ships, low to the gunnels with seal pelts, a few miles off Bragg's Island.[50]

In 1977 and 1978, the clergy of six religious denominations gave official support to the sealers in two ways: by proclamation, and by participation at community meetings. As external protest intensified, Newfoundlanders sought justification from every available source. The involvement of the clergy is significant because, as the intermediaries between lay people and a higher power, their authority is considerable. Whereas the motives of politicians are occasionally suspect, the clergy are believed to be immune from corruption.

Religious differences were put aside in an ecumenical approach to the sealing controversy. At a public meeting in St. Anthony on 14 March, 1977, religious leaders joined Provincial Fisheries Minister, Walter Carter, in defending the hunt before an audience of journalists, protesters and local residents. The clergy pledged their wholehearted support behind the sealers, and reasoned their presence in this way: "The church is involved . . . to show by our presence and our words . . . our common concerns and our common mind an official position on the sealing industry as far as the church is concerned."[51] They appeared again to conduct a short service of prayer at the sealers' send-off in St. John's on 5 March, 1978. The fleet was blessed and divine guidance was publicly invoked. The singing of the hymn, "Eternal Father, Strong to Save," emphasized the hazards faced by sealers: "O hear us when we cry to Thee/ For those in peril on the sea."

A report stating that Franz Weber had requested Pope Paul to take a position vis-à-vis the hunt ("Only an intervention by the Holy See could incite Canada to renounce its decision which dishonors humanity"[52]) infuriated many and perhaps stimulated counter-protest expressions such as this:

In the meantime
Onward Christian sealers
Sailing to the Front.
Don't let the protesters
Interrupt the hunt.[53]

In an article in the Clerical Caller, the newsletter of the Newfoundland conference of the United Church of Canada, Reverend Arthur S. Butt reminisced about his own experience at the Front and concluded by admonishing those who sought to interfere: "May God forgive the protesters for the dispensation of their false propaganda and may He bless the Sealers who will prosecute the 1978 seal hunt and prosper the work of their hands."[54]

CHAPTER II

RHETORICAL STRATEGIES OF COUNTER-PROTEST

This chapter attempts to identify and describe characteristic features of counter-protest and argues that preferred rhetorical strategies are: (1) emergent through time, and (2) derivative of shared geographic and historical experience.

Outrage, frustration and pride form the emotional core of sealing counter-protest. Rebuttal takes a variety of forms, but the most common are these:

> Objection to interference
>
> ". . . the campaign is a . . . hatchet job of almost historic proportions . . . the image of the Province is being smeared falsely and viciously."[1]
>
> Discrediting opponents
>
> "It is time the self-appointed guardians of the herds stopped their interference and went home. One wonders if the furor would be the same if seal pups were lobster-shaped and had cod faces."[2]
>
> Retaliation
>
> "I wouldn't think twice about giving them a bash on the side of the head . . ."[3]
>
> Assertion of rights
>
> "We will not let anybody from anywhere do anything that would destroy our traditional values . . . we're fighting for our very survival in Newfoundland."[4]

Retaliation threats are particularly revealing expressions because they reflect a broad spectrum of attitude towards the protesters and the controversy in general.

> We will fight a battle which will make the one we held in March, 1977, look like a Sunday school picnic.[5]

As Premier Moores says,

> 'The time has come' to stop this gang dead in their tracks and not permit them any accommodations, no fuel for their 'copters, no assistance whatever and certainly no co-operation in any shape or form; only harass them without violence.[6]
>
> They should be arrested and for punishment made to eat overripe seal meat three times a day for 30 days. Then they should be dipped in a vat of permanent pink dye and shipped off home.[7]

One must be careful not to assume that a sarcastic threat implies a light-hearted or amused view of the intruders. Often the most preposterous statement is the product of prolonged frustration and hostility.

> 'I'd like to have them out here on the pans so I could drown 'em all,' said Mercer Cullimore of Little Catalina, amid general laughter from his mates as he was interviewed on the ice. 'They never saw a seal in their life except a tame one. If they seen a good dog hood* they'd never stop running.'[8]

Esoteric threats such as the above attempt to discredit the protesters and imply that sealers are tougher and more experienced, and therefore their cause will ultimately triumph. At the Viking Motel in March, 1977, Bill Short told Brian Davies: "Mr. Davies, you are late for your appointment on the Front. If you were a sealer, you'd starve on the Front this morning."[9]

As suggested previously, the justification for and rationalization of the hunt has relied on five basic arguments, yet the dispute is fuelled by another equally vital issue: the moral integrity of sealers, and by extension, of all Newfoundlanders. Charges of cruelty and barbaric behaviour are countered with the suggestion that protesters are ignorant, publicity-seeking individuals who are meddling in matters that do not concern them.

Ironically, the attack on sealers was initiated by a native-born Newfoundlander. In 1960, an article appeared in Canadian Audubon written by Harold Horwood, an active conservationist. His description of the hunt as a "tragedy on the whelping ice" was laden with emotional imagery: "As dawn breaks over the frozen sea it reveals a scene of primitive barbarism: men wallowing in blood and fat, laying about them with their gaffs among the infant Harp seals that have been deserted by their panic-stricken mothers . . ."[10] Horwood refers to the traditional "Bloody Decks" toast as "symbolic of the barbarity with which the seal hunt is conducted." The 1964 Artek film, shot in the Magdalen Islands and later broadcast on Canadian television, aroused considerable public indignation and paved the road for multiple "save the seal" campaigns.

> . . . a crude Ceasarian performed on a pregnant mother seal hit on the head, the baby torn out of her body, the pup skinned without even stunning it, the mother animal regaining consciousness while all that happened --everywhere laughing, joking, swearing men in parkas and fur-trimmed overalls hitting baby seals and mother

---

*A mature Hooded seal.

> animals alike--hitting, kicking, slitting throats, tearing the furry skins off dead, half-dead, dying animals . . . a symphony of horror, a ghastly chorus of the damned which filled every corner of the sealing area--eery noise creating a fitting background of sound to the slow advance of red blood over the white expanse . . .[11]

Sensational journalism, corresponding to the European and North American concern with conservation and the emerging environmental movement, made the seal hunt a particularly vulnerable target. The issue was moral dynamite; with a few pictures and an impassioned appeal on the seals' behalf, protesters were able to raise incredible sums of money with relatively little effort. As the controversy aged, inflammatory speeches discrediting sealers were gradually abandoned by Davies and Greenpeace, but Newfoundlanders would continue to respond to such labels as "savage barbarians." Newfoundland Premier, Frank Moores, opened his remarks at a Washington, D.C., news conference by stating: "No one likes to be the subject of innuendo and slander. No people like to be branded as sadistic insensitive, ruthless barbarians . . . (Even) your Congress has fallen prey to half truths and simplistic statements concocted by protest groups."[12]

Recognizing that blood and the slaughtering of animals is always an unpleasant sight, defenders of the hunt make frequent analogies to commercial abattoir operations: "I have never seen a seal killed in a barbarous manner--whether by gun or by a club. The scene of the kill is no more pleasant than that of the abattoirs I have visited, but it is just as humane.[13] Tom Hughes, the Executive Vice-President of the Ontario Humane Society, spent many years studying different techniques of animal slaughter. He acknowledges that the hunt is a "repulsive spectacle," with potential for abuse by inexperienced hunters, but he defends it as humane and legitimate. Hughes' participation in the pro-sealing campaign lent it credibility as his involvement began while he was still a member of the S.P.C.A. in British Columbia. His initial purpose was to investigate the issue of cruelty. While on tour with the Newfoundland Government campaign in 1978, Hughes made the following assessment: "The greatest immorality in the seal hunting controversy has been the reckless, indiscriminate, deliberate campaign of racial discrimination and hatred which has been deliberately fostered against the people of Newfoundland and of Canada by groups of individuals whose primary aim is to raise funds, particularly in the United States and Europe.[14]

Reactions by Newfoundlanders to charges of barbarism and cruelty vary considerably. Some are indignant and angry: ". . . your dastardly attempt to scuttle one of our industries, and few we have, is nothing short of sabotage."[15] A less-impassioned appeal, but nevertheless a firm denial, is offered by a sealer:

> I have a great appreciation for nature. I respect nature and learn from it. I am amazed by it. For Brian Davies to call Newfoundlanders a bunch of maniacs, barbarians and savages is so wrong. There are no more sympathetic people on earth than Newfoundlanders. If I were to kill a seal and didn't kill it clean, then I would feel for it. The majority of fishermen I know feel that way. When you kill something, blood has got to flow. To the people who don't understand, it looks terrible. It makes you look like a savage, but it is the right thing to do when it is done right.[16]

A non-sealer was angered sufficiently to respond to the cover illustration of Weekend Magazine of March 11, 1978. The impressionistic sketch of a person wearing a white fur coat smeared with blood, was circulated throughout Canada, and perpetuated the emotionalism of the sealing issue:

> The morning of Saturday, March 11, began in an uneventful almost boring manner. As is wont of a savage, and in accordance with my proscribed role as a Newfoundlander, I spent the early hours ravaging the countryside and torturing all the animals in sight. A trail of blood stretching to the horizon, the extermination of several species of wildlife, and the gratification of a job well done were my just rewards. After kicking the cat 30 yards onto the nearest high-voltage wires, goring the dog with my cane, and tightening the vice on my wife's skull, I settled back to peruse the shining light in the void of journalism, Weekend Magazine . . .[17]

Although 'professional' protesters refrained from making overtly insulting remarks about Newfoundlanders during their stay in St. Anthony, hate letters from distant places poured into the community and to the office of Fisheries Minister, Walter Carter. Some of these were printed in Decks Awash, and others were read on the local CBC television program, Here and Now. A few examples suggest their incendiary nature:

> Sir, . . . you aren't even brave enough to kill anything but baby seals, newly born. Such savagery is unthinkable in a civilized society--but whoever said Newfoundland is a 'civilized society.' You even use clubs to do your savagery: shades of Neanderthal man! . . . I thank God we live far away from you in a civilized land. With contempt for you and shame and embarassment for all humanity. (J.C., III.)

> Dear R.P., . . . I have heard that you are very tired of being labelled a murderer, but 'if the shoe fits, wear it!'

> There is no other title that so aptly fits you and your group of thugs. You obviously have extremely low intelligence . . . (S.W.)
>
> P.C., . . . You poor, poor man! Were you born deformed, lacking the most important quality of all, the one that is supposed to establish mankind as God's most blessed creation? Or were you deformed by others, say ugly, brutal people, perhaps your own parents?
>
> The blind are not as handicapped as you are: those who are crippled can still see beauty and loveliness in the world around them. But you--you poor, poor man! Compared to you the death you harbor in your heart sinks into your groin to render you impotent. Better that such a child sink into eternal darkness than that it exist to pass along the heritage of bloodlust to another generation. (M.B., California).[18]

The ideas expressed in such letters were generally held to be intolerable, and retaliation was directed at Davies, Greenpeace, Weber, and occasionally Brigette Bardot for her activities in 1977. Many counter-protesters did not (or could not) discriminate between the organizations; when Ray Elliott (see Appendix I) was queried about the Greenpeace organization, he dismissed them as a "small religious organization."[19]

Some Newfoundlanders at first thought the protest was a joke: "it was so foolish, coming down to paint the seals."[20] Then followed bitterness: ". . . we are too late by years. The tarnishing of our good name has been done and still is continuing by this so-called conservationist."[21] A sampling of comments show the image held of protesters:

> Yes, there is a problem indeed to rid the world of such scum as there is roaming the earth, however, we can probably see that the P.S.P.G. (punk seal pup group) is fighting a losing battle.[22]
>
> People who do not know the reality of a Newfoundland rural way of life such as movie stars, city slickers, Greenpeacers should stay out of our affairs. A person whose hands have never been dirty or salted by the sea should keep their dainty hands out of it.[23]
>
> Misinformed, cease senseless protesting (signal flags on the port side of the "Norma & Gladys," St. John's harbour, March 5, 1978).[24]
>
> Well, here is a little friendly advice for the little dandies from Chicago. Our sealers are not used to being shoved or pushed around especially when they are trying to make a dollar. They might panic and clobber one of them over the head with a greasy flipper, and the

> headlines of the Telegram would go something like this, 'Greenpeace turns to red conflict as sealer clobbers airline stewardess with greasy, bloody flipper 25 miles southeast of the Offer Wadhams.'[25]
>
> With the end of another seal hunt, Newfoundlanders can revert in the minds of their fellow Canadians from villainous despoilers of white-skinned innocence to the simple-minded rubes that, bless their hearts, refuse to abandon their moon-rock province for the civilized pleasures of Toronto.[26]

STYLE AND LANGUAGE

Rhetoric is designed to persuade, and persuasion requires skillful manipulation of language, values and sentiment. As rhetoric, counter-protest is culturally specific in that the strength and comprehensibility of its appeal relies on shared experience.

The frequent use of the first person plural form, "we," serves to reinforce group allegiance as well as to point out the separate worlds of Newfoundlanders and outsiders:

> No, we are working, fighting people,
> We have struggled and are proud of our name
> So to you who do us wrong
> Why come to where you don't belong?[27]

Reference to specific incidents and the elaboration of stereotypes give the expressions a highly esoteric quality. A good example was the sign raised aboard the "Martin Karlsen" upon its return from the ice in 1977: "Greenpeace Special: Flippers and Carcasses." The ship had been involved in a newsworthy escapade by Paul Watson, the Greenpeace leader who hand-cuffed himself to the loading winches. The banner displayed later in St. John's demonstrated the crew's attitude toward the incident. As a mild form of ridicule, it suggested ineptitude on the part of those who attempted to interfere, and signalled victory for the sealers.

Personal experience narratives and reminiscences are frequently relied on as valid counter-protest testimony. In contrast to protesters and the government, who seek to convince the public with statistical documentation, individuals are more likely to argue through example. This preference for oral testimony is part of the seafarer's tradition--survival at sea requires careful observation and an ability to make decisions under adverse conditions. Such skills are acquired through personal experience and listening to the experiences of fellow fishermen. It is not surprising, therefore, that these protesters and counter-protesters cannot sustain an argument with each other.

Because counter-protest is defensive, expressive forms stress the negative qualities of opponents. Stereotyping becomes useful as a vehicle for venting hostility and frustration: ". . . these pampered city slickers that a day's hard work would kill."[28]

Stereotypes appear in a wide spectrum of contexts--they may be used as serious referents, or they may be used as the focal points for sarcasm and in-group humour: "Despite Moores' efforts, it looks like these bedlamers from the protest groups will be back at the Front again this year, whelping new propaganda stories which should show us the error of our barbaric ways. Perhaps only when we die and go to that great ice pan in the sky will we get to hunt our seals in peace."[29] In addition, stereotypes function like proverbs in that both "sum up a situation, pass judgement, recommend a course of action, or serve as secular past precedents for present action."[30] As stylized responses to recurrent situations, stereotypes are integral features of counter-protest. They are aggressive assertions that define a group's identity _vis-à-vis_ a threatening group. Since persuasive appeals draw strength from arguing with the familiar, stereotypes, precisely because they are based on 'everyday knowledge,' are useful rhetorical devices. They do not require explication to members of the group who employs them.

In Newfoundland, stereotypes about the anti-sealing protesters flourish because there is minimal face-to-face interaction with them. Brian Davies, Greenpeace, and other protesters spend a short time in the province, and when they are present, they remain mostly in St. Anthony at the tip of the Northern Peninsula. The majority of Newfoundlanders rely on the media for news of activities at the Front and so their opinions are based on second-hand (and often editorialized) reports.[31]

Vernacular language in counter-protest confirms that it is directed at promoting internal group solidarity. Thus, Newfoundland terms such as swilers, bedlamers, gaff, and others are familiar to insiders, but are strange to the ears of most mainlanders.

An earlier examination of the seal fishery made this crucial point (though leaving it unexplored): "It is interesting to note that their use of such terrestial terminology as 'ice fields,' 'seal meadows,' and 'harvesting' in describing the ice-scape and sealing operation itself suggests that the sealers perceived the ice-floes to be a seaward extension of their terrestial resource base."[32] This idea was repeated by the President of the Newfoundland Fishermen, Food and Allied Workers Union, Richard Cashin, during a televised interview on 14 March, 1977: ". . . our raison d'être . . . is to harvest the sea."[33] If one is familiar with the barren landscape of Newfoundland ("the rock" is often used to describe the island), it is understandable why the sea is viewed as a resource for cultivation and management. This is not to suggest mastery, but it does imply an appreciation of the inhabitants' historical and contemporary dependence on the sea. Through language, Newfoundland's isolation by the sea is phenomenologically reduced. Agricultural terms such as "harvest" and "bumper crop" invest a sense of human control over an otherwise capricious resource.

Respected human attributes are frequently revealed in verse and prose expressions. The suggestion that sealers are cruel is denied emphatically, and references to wives and family back at home reinforce the argument of economic necessity.

The work ethic receives hearty approval and the notion of accepting money from wealthy foreign entrepreneurs is treated with scorn.[34] Swilers are portrayed as tough, God-fearing family men who accept responsibility for earning their livelihood despite occupational dangers and hardship: ". . . But the money earned by honest sweat/ is better than the dole."[35] Newfoundlanders are proud of their image as being a friendly and hospitable people, and they resent one-sided publicity which ignores this valued trait: ". . . Now we always have a welcome for anyone on earth/ To come and spend some time with us to see just what we're worth.[36]

The ability to laugh and find humour in even the most desolate circumstances is another aspect of island life. Cyril Poole explored the question of Newfoundland humour in a lecture entitled, "The Soul of the Newfoundlander," in which he suggested that there is an intimate connection between humour and the "daily encounter with the sea."

> . . . to encounter the untameable sea is to meet some of the most primordial and inviolable laws of nature face to face, eye-ball to eye-ball. Now it has struck me that the incidents and stories that tap the deepest springs of Newfoundland humour are precisely those in which a living thing or person, preferably a Newfoundlander, breaks or bends those laws.[37]

Certain comic aspects of the protest are highlighted by Joe Connolly's book of cartoons, On the Front (see excerpts, pp. 30-32). In the following verse, Brian Davies is mocked for his inability to cope as cleverly on the ice as the sealers whom he attempts to harass:

Now the sea is running mountains high
It made his stomach ache
he is not like Newfoundlanders
the sea he could not take.[38]

Survival in the face of isolation created a people noted for their independence and self-sufficiency. They become puzzled and then angered by unsolicited interference.

The counter-arguments offered are directed to exposing hypocrisy on the part of protesters. They highlight some of the special concerns of open-line shows and letters-to-the-editor columns: abortion, crime, poverty, race relations, hunger etc. The motives of 'do-gooders' (from the United States, France, Great Britain, and Germany) who seek to save seals, rather than attend to problems of their own, are suspect:

> . . . Well, extinction is a word that is used so
> I've heard,
> As a way to stop that war in [Northern] Ireland.[39]

Newfoundlanders were angered with both the Federal and Provincial Governments for their reluctance to take a firm stand against the protesters. Many felt the prevailing policy to ignore the protesters was politically naive, and the PRO was formed for precisely that reason.[40]

> Where's our MPs? - Our Government? Why don't they
> intervene
> To prevent our white coats from awearin' o' the
> green.[41]

Confrontations are out-of-the-ordinary events. They are discomforting because normal patterns of activity are disturbed, and whenever routine or tradition is challenged by external forces, there is an obligation to defend them. There are a variety of ways to achieve this end, and many Newfoundlanders, with their long (cultural) tradition of verse-making, use it as an expressive coping strategy.

> We think of poetry (or any self-consciously voiced expression) as the adopting of various strategies for the encompassing of situations. These strategies size up the situations, name their structure and outstanding ingredients, and name them in a way that contains an attitude toward them.[42]

Attitude, or point of view, is conveyed through tone (serious, satirical, sentimental, etc.) and emotion (anger, compassion, pride, etc.). Therefore, with regard to the composer's intent, a thematic analysis of counter-protest is only partially instructive.

THREE STRATEGIES

Collectively, three general attitudes towards the sealers, protesters and the entire controversy are discernible: (1) celebratory and condemning; (2) sympathetic and reproachful; and (3) facetious and satirical. I will discuss these attitudes as three rhetorical strategies.

Few verses or songs belong to an exclusive category; in fact, the tone frequently shifts within the compositions. Because they are typically spontaneous and reflexive, it is doubtful that this switching is deliberate, but it is indicative of the ambivalence which surrounds the issue.

There is a partial correspondence between classical rhetoric and the rhetorical strategies of counter-protest. Speeches of praise and blame (epideictic rhetoric) in classical rhetoric were concerned with honour and dishonour; they argued in the present, using existing conditions as the source of their persuasive appeal. Deliberative rhetoric was advisory; through encouragement or dissuasion, a future course of action was recommended. Questions of advantage or injury were paramount. The third type, forensic or judicial rhetoric, argued from past precedent. Through accusation or defense, the primary concern was with justice and injustice.[43]

In sealing counter-protest, the verses which I have labelled celebratory/condemning are similar to the classical epideictic and forensic forms. They praise and blame, accuse and defend. Verse-makers invoke the past, relying on tradition to lend authority and legitimacy to the issue. Sealers are praised and accorded honour, while protesters are scorned as dishonourable zealots. The anti-hunt campaign is viewed as a terrible injustice to the people of Newfoundland. Protest from Britain is particularly antagonizing since Newfoundlanders have not forgotten the heavy losses they suffered while fighting for Britain in the two world wars.

The intent of deliberative rhetoric, and its mode of persuasion, corresponds with verses on the sympathetic/reproach continuum. Emotions are mollified and the tone is solicitous rather than accusing. The audience is entreated to believe that the hunt is justified because sealers are only doing what they must to earn a living. Protesters are reproached for mis-directing their energies towards seals when there are many other urgent social evils which require attention. Advantages versus injury--to the economy of Newfoundland, the culture and the environment--if the hunt is ended, are deliberated in verse format. Rationalization is paramount, and the persuasive means is evidence rather than emotional charges.

Celebratory/Condemning

The most common rhetorical strategy is to praise the sealers and condemn the protesters. Sealers are depicted in idealized terms: "humble, hard-working," "Christian, salt of the earth," and so on. In contrast, protesters are characterized as: "parasites," "Charlatans," "slickers," "gripes," "busy bodies," among others. Sealers represent all that is good and valued, while protesters are destructive and malicious. There are occasional heroes--Cashin and Hughes--but more often the sealer is the ordinary man who deserves praise for the very fact that he does not seek glory but attends to his own business. Considerable energy is devoted to reducing the stellar images of Bardot, Davies, Weber, and Greenpeace to symbols of treachery and evil.

Anger and disgust are the prevailing emotions in this type of verse. The tone is serious, defensive and authoritative. The message is straightforward and declamatory. There are no indications that the author is willing to listen to other arguments; his mind is set, judgement has been passed, and the issue is closed.

Sympathetic/Reproachful

The second strategy is less forceful. It appeals to the audience by invoking images of the hard-working sealer who goes to the ice not for the adventure but out of necessity. References to pregnant wives and hungry children are contrasted with reproach aimed at protesters who are wealthy enough to charter helicopters and hire starlets. Hypocrisy is emphasized, and rhetorical questions are asked of the self-proclaimed seal saviours: "So to you who do us wrong, Why come to where you don't belong?"[44]

Much of the content informs about the circumstances of the hunt in an attempt to rectify the tarnished image of Newfoundlanders. There is an appeal for compassion: "Pride from people they do not know, Why do they come and treat us so?"[45] Many of the verses are pleas for fairness, and examples of social evils and other injustices are included for their contrastive value: "They say we're awfully cruel because we kill the seal. I'd like to explain to them just how we Newfies feel."[46]

Facetious/Satirical

The third rhetorical strategy juxtaposes solemnity with humour in its treatment of the protesters, thus helping to alleviate the anxiety and frustrations that inevitably accumulate after years of protest. Facetious/

satirical verses express hostility in a socially acceptable way. By assuming a playful attitude, composers of this type of rhetoric assert and maintain control over an otherwise disturbing situation. A related characteristic of satirical verse is:

> Like gossip, satirical songs are a private view of affairs of public interest, loaded with special pleading. Unlike gossip, on the other hand, they make public a private assessment of a situation in a candid manner that only a song can do. The satirical songmaker walks the thin line between amusement and libel.[47]

The lack of sustained humour in early counter-protest verses might be considered a measure of the public attitude towards the controversy. Several compositions open with facetious verses or suggestions, only to switch back to serious argument in their conclusion. Obviously the issue is perceived to be too vital and threatening to be treated lightly.

There is evidence, however, that the media have been instrumental in reversing this attitude. By 1978, reporters and commentators began to refer to the March confrontation in St. Anthony as the "annual circus." The gathering of international journalists, screen celebrities, politicians, and academics transformed the whitecoat hunt into a media event. Where once the skill and bravery of sealers preoccupied the imagination of poets and reporters, the antics of protesters now took priority.

The emergence of "Codpeace" (Ch. 3) in 1979, suggests that Newfoundlanders are beginning to feel more confident about their efforts to counter the protest. So, too, do the cartoons of Joe Connolly reproduced on the following pages. They incorporate the arguments used in other expressive forms such as verses, letters and radio calls, but their persuasive function may be secondary to esoteric amusement.

The cartoon (p. 30), depicting a scene at the ice, is a satirical comment on the motives of protesters. It confirms a point made earlier: that the general public does not make clear distinctions between the various protest organizations. Greenpeace is a non-profit environmental corporation, whereas Brian Davies' International Fund for Animal Welfare is a taxable organization. Although the financial benefits of the protest is a disputable point, the majority of Newfoundlanders believe there is money to be made in the effort. "The protectionists, parasitic in the sense they live off public funding, who never had to fight the elements for a living or were born into an upper class family, see the seal as a pet, while in reality, he is a nightmare to fisherman, destroying his chances to obtain the luxuries that other people obtain so readily."[48]

The negative stereotyped image of protesters, and Greenpeace in particular, is obvious in this next cartoon (p. 31). It is culturally esoteric in that Greenpeace enjoys a positive image in the United States and in many regions of Canada. Their appearance, described by Junior Abbott as "female people" referring to slim, long-haired protesters, offers a sharp contrast to the rugged image of sealers. The expensive apparel and gear worn by Greenpeace members are a source of ridicule.

The idea that protesters are ignorant about seals and Newfoundland life, despite articulate press releases arguing their knowledgeability, is a common theme: "Greenpeace have a very appropriate name as they are really green as far as knowledge of the seals are concerned."[49]

Joe Connolly's interpretation of the common argument ". . . if the seal pup had a face like a pig, the Davies types would not be involved"[50] is amusing in an ironic sense. The image of the whitecoat seal, with its big brown eyes, has been exploited by protesters to elicit sympathy and donations, while other, less appealing species have been neglected by activists. The common reference to pig faces is an interesting comparison, and is related to the assertion that sealing is more humane than commercial abattoir operations that produce pork and beef. Another inference of the first cartoon on the next page is that sealers will eventually outwit the protesters with their guile and perserverance.

As argued, counter-protest expressions are reactionary rather than innovative. The second cartoon on the next page demonstrates this quite clearly in that it documents an actual protest event. On 18 March, 1978, Greenpeace President, Dr. Patrick Moore, was arrested for obstructing the seal hunt by sitting on a whitecoat in order to protect it from the sealers' clubs. Department of Fisheries officials warned Moore to move, but he refused and was charged for the offense.

(Cartoons reproduced with permission from Jesperson Printing, Ltd., On the Front, by Joe Connolly, 1978.)

CHAPTER III

VERSE-MAKERS AND THEIR VERSES

Protest and counter-protest songs document strife between conflicting interest groups. Socio-economic differences often divide a population; the sealing controversy, however, proved to be an occasion when people relinquished their class identities and fought for a common cause. The counter-protest stems from a feeling of cultural unity inspired by external threat, and Newfoundlanders, with their long tradition of verse-making, turned to song and poetry to communicate these strong, almost chauvinistic sentiments.

Some of the verses of counter-protest were written as songs, but the majority were written as poetry. They belong together because they share an expressive urgency. In this instance, a formal, generic classification is secondary to the message and its presentation.

I have used two somewhat arbitrary criteria for arranging these verses. The first divides the verses according to the author's history of composing specifically to communicate a message or point of view, and the second involves the predominant rhetorical strategy chosen by the author to express this message. Although there is inevitable overlap between each of these criteria, this arrangement does serve to account for the distinguishing features of this material.

One of my initial hypotheses could not be validated through the data I received. I speculated that the degree of personal involvement with sealing (or the protest) would affect the tone and emphasis of composition. Only two contemporary poets are ex-sealers (Goobie and Menchions); a few have grandfathers, fathers, brothers, or other relatives who went to the ice; but most verse-makers have become acquainted with sealing through recollections of former sealers from their home communities. Several mentioned Cassie Brown's book, Death on the Ice,[1] as an influence on their attitudes. Although the book was not published until 1972, it has become a classic portrait of the hardships endured in former times and serves as a sharp rebuttal to protesters who charge sealers with being cruel and unfeeling hunters.

Most of the verse-makers can be classified as amateur, although several have received recognition through previous publication or public performances. On the one hand, there is Mrs. Sheardown, who claims to have written only two poems in her life, and on the other, there is Ron MacEachern who has been heard on national radio.

To my knowledge, only three persons have written more than one counter-protest song or verse. MacEachern wrote two short songs (see Professional Performers). Nish Collins, who writes the "Rhymes of the Times" column for the St. John's Daily News, uses current events and issues as the source for his rhyming commentaries. Michael Butler, a retired school teacher, writes poems for many occasions, and the sealing dispute inspired at least four complete poems and a stanza, all of which appeared in the Evening Telegram. He is able to switch from narrative, descriptive poetry ("The Sealers' Send-Off") to more subjective, evaluative moods ("The Greenpiece Intrusion").

The means by which I gained access to this material may also shed light on the poets' views of their status and ability as verse-makers. In February, 1978, I submitted letters to the two St. John's newspapers and eleven other provincial papers, as a means to locate authors of songs or poetry that were composed since 1957 and that dealt with the sealing controversy. I received four replies in the mail. Only one was unsigned; the paper was torn at the top, and I can only surmise there was some kind of message which, at the last minute, the author decided to omit. Fortunately, the March 9, 1978, issue of the St. Anthony Polaris News reprinted the poem and identified the author as Albert March of Stephenville, and I was able to contact him and thank him for sending me a copy of the poem. Other poems I heard in performance. Mary MacIsaac recited her "Swilin' '77" at the LSPU Hall (St. John's) in November, 1977, during the "Good Entertainment" festival, and Ron MacEachern was a guest on Sylvia Tyson's "Touch the Earth" radio program. Ron sang both of his pro-sealer songs and explained to the audience how he came to support the hunt after carefully considering both sides of the issue. The other poems I discovered by chance, reading through back issues of newspapers, talking with the Mummers Troupe (I found Phoebe Bonnah's poem posted on their office wall), or contacts through friends (Tom Goobie's, "Brian Davies' Song," and Pat Sulley's, "Coffee on the Last Day").[2]

The authors of the verses that I had collected on my own were extremely co-operative when I contacted them for permission to include their work in this study. Because many of the poets did not live in St. John's, I devised a questionnaire (see pp. 82-85) to accompany a more personal and explanatory covering letter. The questionnaire asked for information about the author's previous writing experience, the degree of his involvement with the sealing issue, his view of the protesters and efforts to counter the attack, and about his perception of his role as a composer/performer. Since several of the replies were quite detailed and explicit, I have reprinted them with the verses because they contribute to a better understanding of the counter-protest theme.

The first section consists of verses and commentary by amateurs whose work has been shared with family and friends, for the most part. This is by far the largest group (13 examples). These verses are then sub-divided by tone, which in effect, suggests the author's point of view. There are celebratory/condemning poems, and sympathetic/reproachful verses as well. Several contain facetious/satirical stanzas, but not one author used this strategy consistently through the composition. Anonymous or unidentified compositions have been included within these classifications, since the author's reluctance or refusal to acknowledge his work might be assumed to mean that the message is more vital than any potential recognition.

The verses of Michael Butler, Mary MacIsaac and Angus Lane comprise the second group. Each of these individuals has been an active verse-maker for a number of years, and all have had the satisfaction of either publishing, performing or recording for a public audience. Although their self-evaluations may differ, they have all known the satisfaction of unsolicited approval from sources beyond their immediate sphere of acquaintances.

Ron MacEachern, Pat Sulley and Gary O'Driscoll are professional performers as well as writers. They are self-conscious about the thematic content of their songs and they acknowledge that audience receptivity is one of their primary considerations in selection and performance of certain songs.[3] The lyrics of Pat Sulley's "Coffee on the Last Day" are the most personal and reflective of the entire collection, but I include them because they belong to this period, and they validate my contention that counter-protest is recognizable by its emotional, value-laden tone rather than by a narrative catalogue of discontent.

The fourth group are unlikely companions, and in some ways, I feel uncomfortable with this division. I have grouped Art Scammell, Nish Collins, John Crosbie and Miller Ayre together on the basis of their public status and access to the media. Nish Collins is the only one among them to earn his living from regular composition, and Art Scammell is a well-known writer. John Crosbie is an elected politician who describes his occasional verse-making as "doggeral"[4] for the amusement of his family and friends. His jest with Brigette Bardot was read publicly in Parliament and later reprinted in the St. John's Daily News. He is appreciated by many for his loyalty to Newfoundland, and is one of the few consistent voices for the province heard at the national level. Miller Ayre is an articulate St. John's businessman who has been angered sufficiently by the protest to make a public counter-protest plea.

AMATEUR POETS

Verses of Celebration and Condemnation

In these verses protesters are accused of being unjust, hypocritical, and agents of destruction for purposes of self-gratification. In sharp contrast, the sealers are depicted as humble, hard-working men who go to the ice for the sake of their families' welfare. There are implicit social distinctions--the protesters are considered to be members of a wealthy elite class, men who have the means and leisure to engage in antics far from their home community. The sealer is the "common man," whose life is a continuous struggle to earn the basic necessities for survival. The language is blunt, the sentiment defiant. The controversy is a battleground and there is no room for compromise.

(Untitled)

In the meantime
Onward Christian sealers
Sailing to the Front
Don't let the protesters
Interrupt the hunt.[5]

M. S., Bell Island

The unidentified author of this short verse was reacting to the cover of the March 11, 1978 Weekend Magazine. In an angry letter, M. S. contrasts the morals of Newfoundland sealers with those of the protesters: "As for Brigette Bardot protesting the seal hunt, it would be more to the point, if she would protest the slaughter before birth. Imagine the human children who will never see earth. Thousands of human lives are being taken away each day, mostly because people want to hide their sons. At least the seal hunters are not guilty of that. The seal hunt is once a year, not day after day (like the killing of human fetus) . . ."[6]

(Mrs.) Jean Hiscock, Deer Lake

The Seal Hunter

He's called the cruel sealer
He's one of a hardy race
He's dressed in a coat of misery
And worry haunts his face

In his clammy hands he holds the club
and raises it above his head.
He sees the bloody ice around him
And the little pups lying dead.

But in his mind there's a picture
Of his pregnant wife on shore
Of his children, their empty stomachs waiting.
And he hesitates no more.
Danger lurks around him
The shifting pans, the biting cold
But he thinks of the things he'll buy for his home
When all the pelts are sold.

He thinks of the Greenpeace Foundation
Eating their chicken and pork
And he hates the way they condemn him
For the sealmeat on his fork.

May the devil take tormentors
To a place where it's nice and hot.
And let them repent for their own selfish acts
While they're roasting in his pot[7]

The letter accompanying this poem is reprinted below.

February 22, 1978

Dear Ms. Lamson,

I am flattered that you wish to use my poem, "The Seal Hunter," in your Master's thesis, and permission is, of course, granted. I was as surprised as anyone when my poem appeared in the Newfoundland Herald for the second time. I also felt quite good about it. I support the seal hunt, and as a mother of three children, as well as being a "drab" housewife, there was little else I could do to show my support.

Before I start to answer your questions, I'd like to give you an idea of how I felt and thought as I wrote my poem. I tried to put myself in the position of the sealer, to feel as he must feel about all the horrible things being said about him. I figured that he's a tough guy if he gets out to face the harsh Newfoundland winter on the ice floes. I could just see him there, his coat caked with snow, his face reddened, wrinkled by the sharp wind, his eyes unable to hide the worry. My father was a fisherman and I know he always worried that there wouldn't be enough fish to buy the things we needed, and I imagined the sealer must have similar feelings.

In the second verse his hands are clammy because he doesn't like what he has to do. He is aware of his surroundings. He does not need people like Brian Davies and the others to tell him what's going on. This is a necessary way of life for him, and nothing anyone can say or do is going to change the way he thinks or feels.

The whole while he is on the ice his family is never far from his mind. For them, he faces the unpleasantness, the danger; they are his source of strength and endurance.

He wants the protesters of the hunt to know that it is not all enjoyment being stranded on ice pans in freezing weather. He needs the money the pelts will bring, maybe to buy food, or maybe for a needed piece of furniture, or maybe even to put a roof over his family's head. Surely some of those who oppose the hunt eat chicken, pork, lobster, beef, and flesh from other living things. Why should they condemn him because he enjoys a meal of seal meat?

In his frustration and anger the sealer wishes they would all go to hell. In fact, he is almost certain they'll all end up there. He hopes the devil is ready to torture them. He'd like to watch them squirm as they regret their part in the seal hunt. As far as he's concerned, they're just doing it for personal recognition anyway. There are, after all, many ignorant people in the world, who have no idea what it's like to live in a small Newfoundland outport where employment is scarce. Such people (and most of them are well-to-do) eagerly finance ego-trips for people like Paul Watson and the others who get to travel around the world in the limelight of the countries they visit. They (Greenpeace Foundation and the rest) are not so much concerned with saving the seals and whales and other species as they are with themselves, and with the publicity they get. Many of them get more publicity than the seals do, and that's the way they want it.

(1) I have written other verses about many other subjects. I wrote my first verse when I was in the fifth grade. I enjoy writing about death, uncertainty, nature, and most especially, the sea, the beach, gulls, and fish. The Newfoundland Herald once published one of my poems, "Reason to Remember," a long time ago when it was in newspaper form. Aside from that, none of my verses were previously published.

(2) I write for personal satisfaction. I work out my frustrations on paper. I do not deliberately set out to write a poem--such verse would be strained and unnatural. I write spontaneously. Perhaps something may bother me for weeks, then when I'm making a bed or doing the dishes I may have to grab a pen and write as fast as I can before I forget. If I have to spend more than ten or fifteen minutes on a poem, then it is strained, a kind of forced verse. "The Seal Hunter," was written during a commercial when the "Tommy Hunter" show was on TV. If I could just sit down and write a poem, I'd publish books of poetry, but this way, they have to come to me and I may go weeks without writing a poem. Some days I write three or four.

(3) Few people know about my verse-making. I received most of my publicity in high school. I am (or was) more well-known around my home town (Heart's Delight). I like to write funny and nonsense poems for children. I read them to my children's friends. They ask for copies, and give me kisses.

Those who do know about my verse-making say things like, "I don't know how you do it." I remember reading one which is a particular favourite of mine to a friend, who showed little interest and later said, "Well, now that you've wrote it, what are you going to do with it?" In other words, what's the good of it?

(4) I don't know anyone who has gone to the ice. My father would go out in a boat sometimes with another man, and if they were lucky, they'd shoot a seal or two. It was a source of meat and I used to love it before Brian Davies came along. I resent him because he made the seals seem too human and I can no longer eat seal meat although I love it.

All I know about the seal hunt is from what I've seen or heard on T.V., or read in the papers. My husband tells me he once took part in the seal hunt as a landsmen as a teen-ager. He once had the experience of being stranded on an ice pan with several men. They had to leave pelts behind and jump on slob ice to get to safety. There have been tales of worse experiences. I believe the men kill seals more for the necessity of the money than for the pleasure they get from killing.

(5) I think I answered this question earlier in my letter. They do it mostly for themselves. I'd like to travel--perhaps I should join them and get some unsuspecting ignorant people to support me!

Through their protest they may well destroy the seal hunt. They are bringing the focus of the world on Newfoundlanders and painting a picture of a bunch of barbarians. I wouldn't be surprised if many people think we're cannibals.

(6) Most of the protesters are sensationalists. Many have been taken in by others and know very little about what is really happening.

(7) The seal hunt is very definitely threatened by the protesters.

(8) I really don't know what Newfoundlanders should do to defend the hunt. Maybe we should form groups and visit other countries and point out to them that cruelties exist among them. Perhaps we should ask the ones who finance the hunt to use their funds for a much needy cause, like trying to help people in poorer, developing countries. I wonder if we took pictures and films of poor starving and sick children and placed them around the pictures of baby seals would some people think twice about handing money over to these groups?

(9) I think Newfoundlanders are sufficiently concerned about the future of the seal hunt, but it may be too late by now. Something should have been done when Brian Davies first started it all. We thought it was funny then.

(10) My verses were intended as commentary about the existing situation. I also hoped to arouse the interest of others in the seal hunt. Most people are much too placid about things that really concern them.

(11) The only other way I have expressed my concern about the protesters has been discussing it with family and friends.

Sincerely,
Jean Hiscock

Jean Hiscock is an articulate woman who turns to poetry to express her sentiments. As explained in her letter, her verses are spontaneous and reflexive rather than reflective. "The Seal Hunter" is a compassionate but idealized portrait of an ordinary sealer. The rhetoric belongs to the sympathetic category, but the final stanza is an angry, impassioned statement of condemnation.

The notion that sealers enjoy their work is denied by the imagery of the poem--the sealer looks at the "bloody ice" but, thinking of his family and the requirement to feed and clothe them, "he hesitates no more." Economic necessity and occupational hardship are central arguments, and protesters are scorned for their hypocrisy and greed.

Phoebe Martin Bonnah, Happy Valley (Labrador)

Protesters vs Sealers

There's an awful fuss a-brewing on the ice
should we kill the whitecoat seal and is it right
Davies says we'll go to hell, if we don't stop the kill
and Cashin says that's just where he can go.

So its protesters vs sealers in the fight
and before they club each other to the ice
the motives must be known--whose are false and whose
profound--humble sealer, Greenpeace, or the seal

Miss Bardot do you think those furs you've worn
were weaved for you alone by gentle hands?
and do you think that steak, upon your silver plate
was picked off some plant that grows in France?

Brian Davies do you own leather shoes?
Well that leather had a name, was born and died again
and laid its slaughtered body at your feet.

Oh the people of Great Britain are disturbed
they think there'll be extinction of the herds
well, extinction is a word that is used, so I've heard
as a way to stop that war in (Northern) Ireland.

This world is full of walking contradictions
brave sealers of Newfoundland take heart
the world cannot condemn, you've not acted on a whim
if what you do is what you think is right.[8]

Phoebe Bonnah submitted the above to the Mummers Troupe when she learned they were organizing a production about the sealing controversy. Her initial letter stated, "I would very much like to hear it used as a lyrical ballad. However, I do not write or play music, so it's left to your discretion. I am a Labradorian, who, as you might gather, have strong feelings for and against the issue in question."[9] She has been writing verses for twenty years about "everything that interests me--none of which has been published." Her brother, friends and other relatives hunt seals in Goose Bay.

As for the protesters, Phoebe believes, "their concern for the seals, however misguided, is commendable. However, if the main purpose of the organizations are for monetary gain, then those organizations should be attacked and disbanded. What the protesters accomplish is awareness: awareness of the fact that the seal must not be over-harvested to the point of extinction."[10] She describes her verse-making as personal commentary, written for self-satisfaction and for the enjoyment of her family.

"Protesters vs Sealers," is precisely titled, for Phoebe Bonnah does not rely on the traditional pro-sealing arguments. She is concerned about the image of Newfoundland sealers who, in her opinion, have been unjustifiably maligned while self-righteous protesters are allowed to proceed unchallenged. Her strategy is a series of rhetorical questions, heavily weighted to elicit sympathy for the sealers. Bardot, Greenpeace and Davies are accused of acting irresponsibly. The reference to Cashin is the occasion of his meeting with agitators in St. Anthony in March, 1977.

Albert J. March, Stephenville

(Untitled)

Out of St. Anthony where the seals
run free
There are people out hunting for a
baby,
We must stop this slaughter out on
the ice flow,
These were the words of Miss Bridget
Bardot.

But out on the ice flows there is
more to see,
For there is this guy they call
Brian Davies,
But out on the ice flow us Newfies do hunt,
We're not like you people that's putting it blunt.

We're not like you people who kill
you're own kind,
We don't hunt for pleasure and this
you will find.
We're not like you people that's
putting it blunt,
So mind your own business and
stay out of the hunt.

For out on the ice flows us Newfies
will go,
Hunting for seals off the Labrador
flow.
Like our fathers before us to the
ice they did go.
No, you will never stop us,
Miss Bridget Bardot.

Oh you say what we're doing is not
very nice,
Then I say to you friend, read
Death on the Ice,
For out off St. Anthony us Newfies
will go
To suffer the hard times of wind,
ice and snow.[11]

The author, age twenty-eight, writes verses primarily for personal satisfaction, although he mentioned that several friends have asked for copies. He has been writing for eight years about "history, stories I have heard and about people." He does not know anyone who had been to the ice, but referred to Death on the Ice as an influence: "I feel sorry for the seal hunters, for what they went through and for what they are going through now." The protesters are "people looking for attention," and although he does not believe the future of the seal hunt is threatened by the protesters, March does feel greater efforts should be made to counter the protest.[12]

Albert March was surprised to hear from me and to learn of the publication of his poem in the St. Anthony Polaris News (see p. 34, above). He said he submitted the poem about two months ago to the Progressive Rights Organization, who obviously forwarded it to the newspaper. The copy he sent me was slightly different from the published version, and he explained he did not have a copy of the original so he recalled the poem from memory.

The poem is another rhetorical effort to demonstrate the differences between "them" and "us." The author begins by trying to describe a scene objectively, but he quickly switches in the second stanza, to an assertion of allegiance and condemnation: "We're not like you people that's putting it blunt." The key arguments are tradition and occupational hazard: "Like our fathers before us to the ice they did go," and "Then I say to you, friend, read Death on the Ice." The poem condemns protesters, but makes an effort to arouse sympathy for sealers who, "suffer the hard times of wind, ice and snow."

Madeline Pitts, Dunville (Placentia Bay)

The Sealing Dispute

The seal hunt dies in dear Newfoundland
Because of strangers who come and demand
What excuse can they make?
How many jobs will they take?

Pride from people they do not know
Why do they come and treat us so?
Our livelihood we must work to make,
We did not mean any hearts to break.

A seal may be an animal they want to save,
But why concern, when human life they deprave?
May I be bold to say in jest
They have come not to do what is best.

Are we as heartless as they do claim?
No, we are working, fighting people,
We have struggled and are proud of our name
So to you who do us wrong
Why come to where you don't belong?[13]

Madeline Pitts Spurrell, age twenty, has been writing poetry since grade four. She always kept a diary and hopes someday to write a novel. Several of her verses have been printed in the Newfoundland Herald, for which she has been paid a small honorarium.

Madeline feels angry and indignant at the protesters who are closing down an industry and "wrong-doing Newfoundlanders all over the world." Although none of her relatives were sealers, she sympathizes with them because of the dangers they must face; many have big families, and "there is no guarantee they will come back alive." She has spent a lot of time thinking about the protesters and has devised her own taxonomy of motives: (1) the first group are truly concerned about the seal population; (2) the Brigette Bardots are out for the publicity it will bring them--"they don't give a damn about the seal hunt"; and (3) the Brian Davies of the world who are out for profit.

In a phone conversation, Madeline referred to the issue of human abortion. Why there should be such an outcry for seals and apathy towards human victims, is difficult for her to understand.

This poem belongs to the second rhetorical category of sympathetic/ reproachful verses. "Why do they come here and treat us so,?" is a question many Newfoundlanders asked among themselves, the answer to which has yet to be resolved. Whereas financial profit is the motive most often attributed to protesters, Madeline Pitts gave protesters credit for their conservation concerns: "A seal may be an animal they want to save/ But why concern when human life they deprave?" Again, the familiar closing sentiment is defiant and aggressive: "So to you who do us wrong/Why come to where you don't belong?"

Minnie Haw-Haw (Anonymous)

Freedom, Flags and the Seals

Here's to the band of
liberty
Where people are so
human
That the killing of seals for
a living,
Is a big, loud, crying
shame!
A land where the white
man rules the roost,
Provided his "Mrs." lets
him.

Where the thought of a
black breathing his air,
Is the one thing that really
upsets him.
They're fanatic about their
freedom and flag,
If you meet them they'll
kiss and embrace;
While the poor old Newfies,
who live off their seals,
Are a barbarous, murderous
race.
That land where ladies are
screaming for laws
To murder their unborn
child;
Yet the thought of another
race slaughtering seals,
It's driving those kind people
wild.
Send that dame Lambert up
here to Newfie,
Nothing would give me
more glee,
Than to put her on an
icepan,
And push her out to sea.
And if she wants humanity,
What could be more
humane
Than to pick up old Brian
Davies,
And give him more of the
same?[14]

This is the earliest expression of counter-protest I recovered during my investigation. Oblique references to social problems in the United States are used to recriminate charges of cruelty on the part of Newfoundlanders. There is a sober kind of irony used to counter slanderous accusations, but the final verses are more whimsical, implying a view that the protest could be dispelled by a single act of defiance.

"Freedom, Flags and the Seals" is a facetious effort to discredit protesters who dare accuse Newfoundlanders of slaughtering "baby" seals while ignoring problems in their own country. It is an esoteric verse in the sense that the threat of pushing "that dame Lambert" and setting her adrift on an icepan would only be appropriate to regions where respect for ice and the sea is an indisputable cultural fact.

(Mrs.) Alexandrine Mercer, Topsail

Whitecoats, Greencaps

Going to the seal hunt on a winter's day
Watching all the whitecoats innocent at play,
Just thinking of a green cross fills one with dismay,
What will all the pups do when mama turns away?

Come sealer lads from Twillingate a few nights ago
And told the TV audience what they wished to know,
While over on the mainland, they listened goggle-eyed,
As they heard how many seal hearts our boys bring back
with pride.

Going to the seal hunt on a winter's day,
Watching all the Newfie boys joining in the fray,
Laughing at all the Greenpeacers, and their cries of woe,
As armed with heavy spray guns they jump from floe to floe.

Coming home from the seal hunt on a winter's day
Watching all the baby seals and mothers as they play
Watching all the green caps floating in the bay,
Our witty Newfoundlanders, I know they saved the day."[15]

Mrs. Mercer wrote her poem in 1976, the year Greenpeace threatened to dye the seal pups green in an effort to render the pelts useless to the fur industry. The reference to seal hearts acknowledges a custom that the protesters exploited for shock value, but that for Newfoundlanders is not an act of barbarity. The concluding phrases suggest that Newfoundlanders will outwit the Greenpeace lads who have no experience at the ice and therefore are destined to fail.

The letter which Mrs. Mercer sent in reply to my inquiry about her verse-making and attitudes toward the controversy is reprinted in part.

March 3, 1978

Dear Cynthia,

I am gratified that you wish to use my poem, "Whitecoats, Greencaps," in your Master's thesis . . . about the poem, well, at the time, I must admit it was written in some part frivolously. However, I feel much more strongly about the anti-sealing campaign now, and if I were to write a poem or article again, I would express my feelings and beliefs in no uncertain terms, with little or no frivolity.

For the most part, I see humour in most things which triggers off the desire to write poetry. I have written poems, short stories and articles since my early teens (which is quite some time ago). I have always been a dreamer, preferring painting, writing, and playing the violin to housework and any other down-to-earth occupations.

Why do I compose verses? Mostly for self-gratification and for friends; but if I feel strongly enough about a subject I submit it for publication in the hope it will do some good.

I know no one who has been to the ice. I am not a Newfoundlander (Scottish by birth)--but I married a Newfoundlander and think Newfoundland is a wonderful island.

Regarding Brian Davies and the hangers-on, I have a few ideas of my own as to their motives. It could be the beautiful soulful brown eyes of the whitecoats that touched their hearts--it could be entirely for publicity, or it could be a money-making racket. I have no way of knowing whether any or all of my theories may be right. I do feel that no one should interfere with the Newfoundlanders' means of a livelihood, and I am shocked and disgusted with the way this infamy has grown out of all proportion.

I know it has been said many times before but I'll say it again, we have murderers in our midst all the time, when butchers slaughter calves and lambs simply to provide us with legs of veal and lamb chops. Are people so gullible that they lap all this nonsense up?

I am not an intellectual and I can't see myself belonging to a group of protesters, or being recognized by the government for anything I might write. It is my feeling that Newfoundlanders should resort to more drastic measures. I feel they are not paying enough heed to the far-reaching results of the campaign. It will be too late after the seal hunt is banned or if all the markets are closed to us--both in pelts and seal meat.

"Going to the ice" is a way of life for the hunters. They bring to it the proud tradition handed down through the years.[16]

"Whitecoats, Greencaps" is the most whimsical of all the counter-protest expressions in this collection, but it reflects Mrs. Mercer's attitude in 1976, which still was partially disbelieving regarding the potential threat of the protest. By 1978, she no longer viewed the protest as humorous.

In terms of rhetorical arguments, the poem stresses a competitive theme, with protesters and Newfoundlanders trying to outwit one another with clever schemes. There is a facetious reference to mainland audiences who listen "goggle-eyed" to sealing reports. An emergent sense of pride in esoteric traditions, rather than apology, is evident.

C. M., Eastport

Go Home and Live in Greenpeace

Breathes there a man with head so dense
Who never said, I should have had better sense
To improve on nature I should never try
To spray the whitecoats with green dye

These mother seals before going down,
Circle their puppies round and round
When they get their milk to flow
They saturated the encircled snow.

When they have their pups, so white,
They're supplied with milk for the day and night
While they are hunting away from below
They come and spray the pups with snow.

On their mission they onward go
While the puppies eat milk, dye, and snow.
You can be sure beyond a doubt
These pups are green inside and out.

When the mother seals come back this time
Their little puppies they can nowhere find,
The scent of dye is to them unknown,
And they their little pups disown.

For days and days they hunt around,
But nowhere can their pups be found
That spraying spree would sure suffice
To lose their puppies on the ice.

If on their mission they only should
Come in contact with an old dog hood
Their baseball bats would be of no avail
They'd need their gaffs that seal to kill.

Read, mark and learn the best device,
To kill the seals out on the ice;
One slap with gaff that seal lies dead,
Slap, slap and bang those clubs they made.

And one spray of dye would sure suffice,
To starve those puppies on the ice;
But thanks to God they were forced to cease
And go back home and live in Greenpeace.[17]

This is another poem from 1976, the imagery of which refers to the Greenpeace threat to dye the seal pups. A popular though unsubstantiated belief circulating during this period was that mother seals would abandon their young if they were sprayed. It is an interesting reversal of blame for the fate of the young whitecoats: while protesters condemned the cruel methods used by the sealers, this Newfoundlander countered with the argument that abandonment was far more brutal. Furthermore, there would be no gain for either side.

"Go Home and Live in Greenpeace" is one of the few poems in which seals figure prominently. Because it is (rhetorically) sympathetic towards the pups, I had to re-read the composition several times before deciding it did belong to the category of counter-protest. The poem message cleverly implies that seals rightfully belong to sealers in contrast to protesters who are seen as opponents who will bring harm to the seals. The final verses are unmistakenly defiant, invoking divine sanction of the hunt.

The image of the savage old dog hood appears here as it does in several other counter-protest expressions, implying that physical dangers are still very real. There is also a bitter comment on the prohibition of the gaff. The gaff was banned and replaced by the hakapik as the only legal implement for killing seals. Sealers traditionally relied on the gaff to help them jump from ice pan to ice pan, besides using it as a weapon, and many a seasoned sealer voiced concern about the new regulations.

The concluding lines, "But thanks to God they were forced to cease/ And go back home and live in Greenpeace" were somewhat premature since the protesters returned to St. Anthony in 1977, 1978 and 1979, with little to discourage or obstruct their mission.

Pat Casey, Torbay

Sealer's Battle Song

Well the 1st of March is here again,
It's time for all poor fishermen
To go and risk their lives again out on the frozen foam.
They'll be hounded there by Davies, movie stars and Greenpeace
Why don't those bloody mainlanders leave Newfoundland alone.

Well our sealers now for centuries
have worked the arctic ice floes
And they've lived in constant danger and many men have died,
Now those self-appointed saviours of the seal herds in Vancouver
Disrupt their way of living and try to wreck their lives.

Their pocket books are bulging
With mainland contributions
So they leave their twenty dollar steaks and live it up in style.
They won't talk about abortion, they somehow get the notion
That no one cares for children in this year of the child.

Now the good old U.S. congress
Will send their boys to hound us
They'll call us bloody murderers, send hate mail to our homes.
But I wonder who's the murderers, we don't kill our presidents,
And you won't find dirty skeletons beneath our Newfy homes.

Now no sealer dropped the A Bomb
And wiped out Hiroshima,
He didn't own the napalm that burnt Viet Nam.
And unlike the whitecoat saviours we never kill our neighbours
Cause we're God fearing fishermen from dear old Newfoundland.

Now in Trudeau's just society
Injustice really bothers me
How can Alberta be so rich and Newfoundland so poor.
For Ottawa's enjoyment they cut our unemployment
Now Trudeau wins Toronto and we don't eat no more.

No we can't afford the beefsteaks
Premier Blakeny offered
We've no money in our pockets so we'll kill a seal once more.
If we want a meal of salmon, we'll go to Premier Bennett
Cause Leblanc don't issue licences to Newfies any more.

Now no sealer dropped the A Bomb . . . .[18]

This song was composed while the author was recuperating after a six-month illness and hospitalization. During that time he wrote two other verses, but he isn't certain if he will write any more since he is now working full-time as a propane mechanic.

Pat Casey performed this counter-protest song on the "Here and Now" (CBC-TV) show on 5 March, 1979, the day following the sealers' send-off in St. John's. He had never previously performed publicly, and this occasion came about because he sent a tape to the show's production staff who thought it was expressive of the public mood.

A "Sealer's Battle Song" illustrates the cumulative nature of many counter-protest compositions in that it makes reference to protest events of previous years, such as the appearance of Brigette Bardot in 1977, and the visit of two U.S. Congressmen who observed the hunt in 1978.

The author implies that Newfoundlanders are unjustly harassed, not only by zealous protesters, but also by the Canadian government: the suggestion that Ottawa has turned its back on Newfoundland is argued in the sixth and seventh stanzas. Casey juxtaposes the provincial reliance on seals, to Saskatchewan's beef production and the salmon industry in British Columbia. (LeBlanc is the Federal Fisheries Minister.)

Mr. Casey also believes the protesters are given too much protection by the constabulary, and the only way they will be discouraged is to oppose them at every given chance--at airports, hotels, etc. He doesn't believe the protesters will cause the hunt to be abandoned directly, but worries that sealers will finally get fed up with all the negative publicity and name-calling.

Clayton Menchions, Botwood

(Untitled Song)

Have you heard of Brian Davies?
He's the leader of a gang
Who came down here to Newfie
For to try to put a bann
On the killing of the whitecoats
And anything that moves
Just to make himself more famous
When they tell it in the news.

The way he tries to tell it,
Is that all of us are bad,
Just because we like to follow
The ways our fathers had--
To go to hunt the Whitecoats
As they pass along the coast

To make a few more dollars
And have flipper pie to boast.

And then there are the Greenpeace crowd
You've heard of them I'm sure
You'd think they would reform the world
The way they rant and roar
But they're the same as Davies
And all that Mainland gang
We're better off without them
In good old Newfoundland.

The seals that come along our coast
Are there for the use of man
To help him with his food and clothes
It must have been God's plan
But those people from the Mainland
Are all so rich and wise
They have no use for sealskins
Or even flipper pies.

When Smallwood made Canadians
Of us in forty-nine
He didn't think our way of life
Would be put out of line.
He thought that we would hunt and fish
And do just as we please
But the way it looks to some of us
We'll soon do none of these.

So here's to all the Newfies
Who stand up for all their rights
May they never heed Brian Davies
Nor any of his likes
And when it comes to Greenpeace
Or even Swisse Franz
May they learn to live and let alone
Like we do in Newfoundland.[19]

According to the author, this song was composed for a concert in Botwood in April, 1976, to the same tune as the popular, "Kelligrew's Soiree."

Clayton Menchions, age 55, has been writing songs about "anything that appeals to me" for 35 years. He was born in Bay Roberts, Conception Bay, and he has been a clergyman and a school teacher. His work has never been published, yet he is anxious to share his verse, as demonstrated by his taking the initiative and responding to my newspaper inquiry for sealing songs and poetry.

Clayton, his father and his brother were sealers, though he did not specify whether they were landsmen or went aboard the sealing ships to the Front. His comment was brief but precise: "it was a difficult undertaking and a hard way to make a few dollars." The protesters, in Clayton's view, are out for their own personal gain; "they can get a fat and easy living by their protesting."[20]

One of the familiar arguments--divine sanction--appears in the fourth verse as justification for the hunt. Bitterness towards those who would interfere with an independent people is the closing sentiment: "May they learn to live and let alone/ Like we do in Newfoundland." The reference to Confederation ("when Smallwood [Premier of Newfoundland] made Canadians of us in [nineteen] forty-nine") suggests that hostility towards Mainlanders is long-standing, and nostalgia for a way of life gone by evident. In a sense, this song is a call for action.

Tom Goobie, Old Perlican

The Brian Davies Song

You have heard of Brian Davies
The foolish little man
he left his foolish country
and came to Newfoundland

He thought to stop the seal hunt
but it was more than he could do
to frighten off the captains
and their hearty crew.

He landed in St. Anthony
the nearest to the patch
of pretty little whitecoats
where sealers use their bats

He brought with him helicopters
to make an early start
but the landsmen all surrounded him
and his plane it would not start.

The mounties broke the picket line
and let poor Davies free
he went to follow all his gang
out on the northern sea.

But when he got out on the patch
the ice was all broke up
he never had the nerve enough
to stop the killing of the pups.

The sea was running mountains high
it made his stomach ache
he is not like Newfoundlanders
the sea he could not take.

He brought down Mr. Webers
like wise Miss Bardot
to hold a puppy in her arms
and make a great big show.

They soon got fed up with their game
their gas was getting short
and with a very short said tale
back home they made a start.

Farewell to Mr. Davies
Mr. Weber and Bardot
and don't come back here any more
and land upon our shore.[21]

Tom Goobie, 71 years old, is now retired from his life-long career as a fisherman, during which he went sealing three times. His father was also a sealer. Like Clayton Menchions, his remarks about sealing were brief but to the point: ". . . it was hard work and a means of income," suggesting not the adventure but the reality of the occupation.

This song was written in the spring of 1977 after Tom had seen a televised news program which reported Brian Davies' activities in St. Anthony. He was angry and considered the protesters: "stupid to try to stop Newfoundlanders from killing seals." The closing of the seal fishery, replaced by an imitation-fur industry, is Tom's interpretation of the protesters' motives for interfering. He believes the hunt may be threatened, and that "more ships and more Newfies" should become involved.

"The Brian Davies Song" is the only counter-protest expression I collected which is also a narrative documenting local events. Although Michael Butler's "Sealers' Send-Off" is a narrative poem, it lacks the emotional, argumentative qualities that characterize counter-protest verses. As a localized, event-specific song, it is highly esoteric to Newfoundlanders.

The appearance of Franz Weber and Brigette Bardot as accessories to the 1977 protest was interpreted by many as a publicity gimmick. A photo of Bardot protectively holding a whitecoat pup was printed in Paris Match and other international papers.[22] The print served the protesters' cause but angered Newfoundlanders because it was a fraud. The "pup" was the work of a taxidermist and, as many have argued, it would be impossible to hold a live pup because of its sharp talons.

Tom Goobie concludes his song with a negative command "Don't come back here any more/ And land upon our shore." His view is obviously one of disgust.

Verses of Sympathy and Reproach

Statements that appeal for sympathy and compassion rather than demand it, indicate a rhetorical strategy that is deliberative rather than imperative. There is an effort to inform the protesters why the seal hunt is necessary, and to explain the conditions under which the sealers must struggle to survive. The underlying tone suggests a willingness to abide by natural laws, and the protesters are beseeched to do the same.

The emphasis is on dialogue, as though the authors believe they might be able to persuade the protesters to come to their point of view. Name-calling does not feature to the extent that it did in the first group of poems; instead more energy is devoted to portraying Newfoundlanders as a kindly, unassuming, yet dedicated people. Unfortunately, the audience(s) to whom the poems are directed will probably never see these appeals, but they do function to heighten a cultural identity and enhance group solidarity.

Elizabeth Sheardown, White Horse (Yukon)

The Seal Hunt

Come all you people I'd like you to hear
The story of the seal hunt which took place this year
Now Brian Davies that publicity-seeking man
Called come on gang, let's go to Newfoundland.
You know the seal hunt is about to begin
If we don't make trouble it would be a sin
Those Newfoundlanders are an awful bunch
Why they even eat seal flippers for lunch!

The people of St. Anthony cried what's going on
Who are these people who have come along
They've said to the world, let's put the Newfies down
Because for the ice fields they're outward bound.

Now the life of a sealer is difficult at best
But for hundreds of years have withstood the test
Of the stormy March winds and the treacherous ice floe
That have foundered their ships and sent them below.

The Greenpeace objects is to the killing of seals
Saying this slaughter is useless out on the fields
But their wallets are fat, their stomachs are full
While in their choppers they fly out of the cold.

They don't need this income like the sealers do
And never fed their children with seal flipper stew
Davies quit his job when the money rolled in
From contributors whose sympathies he managed to win.

Now a song writer I know I never will be
But I would be happy if I could help one person see
That the Newfoundland Sealers aren't cruel men
Only do what they must for a living to win.[23]

The letter from Mrs. Sheardown is worth reproducing almost in its entirety because it reveals how an individual can be motivated towards expressive behaviour. In this case, an event that stirred her emotions gave her impetus to write, and the radio and her friends were instrumental in encouraging her to submit the verse as a social expression of counter-protest.

March 23, 1978

Dear Miss Lamson,

Thank you for your very kind letter, it was a very pleasant surprise . . . I have written one other poem and that was on the occasion of the birth of my daughter. I wrote it for a friend with whom I had a wager.

Last Spring (1977), the CBC Morning Side program (Harry Brown and Maxine Cook) sponsored a song contest in which the contestants could write about anything they wished. I had no desire to enter. However, while waiting to pick up my son from school one day, I heard a news broadcast concerning the Seal Hunt, Brian Davies, Greenpeace, etc. It made me so angry I decided to write down what I was feeling. I completed all the verses the same day with the exception of the last one. I completed it the following day, but I was never completely satisfied with it. I read it to several of my friends and they encouraged me to enter the contest. I felt there was little chance of winning because of the controversial subject, but I thought there was a possibility that it might be aired as each week several entries were read on the program. I felt it was a great opportunity to express my views coast to coast. However, it was never read and I was disappointed when I received a form letter thanking me for my entry. I then made copies and sent them to my friends and family in Nova Scotia and Newfoundland. In addition, I called a friend who was a Greenpeace member and read her my poem. She protested strongly saying her group did not object to the Newfoundland sealers but rather the foreign sealers, and that their only interest was protecting the seal from extinction. I pointed out that the Newfoundlanders were bearing the brunt of their objections. Even though she felt my views were not accurate, she agreed that if I was correct than the literature she was receiving from Greenpeace was misleading.

My mother (Mrs. Alva Keeping) was pleased with the poem and said she would place it in the paper this Spring. As I had heard nothing else I thought it had gone unnoticed. Although I had the satisfaction of compliments from my friends, I was disappointed as I had hoped someone would want to include my poem as material in an anti-Greenpeace protest.

I feel that Greenpeace and Brian Davies launched a successful protest in Newfoundland simply because of the very nature of the Newfoundland people (warm and unassuming). Brian Davies had very little opposition in the beginning because Newfoundlanders on the whole do not concern themselves with the outside world. I believe that they truly believed that no one would brand them as a brutal and cruel people. However, by the time they realized that this was actually happening, Greenpeace and Brian Davies had already made enormous strides (unchallenged) in convincing the world that this was the case. I feel that the Seal Hunt is threatened by Greenpeace because they play on the emotions of people like my friend who now regard the baby seal as something akin to the human baby. These same people would balk at the idea of eating baby beef if they were constantly reminded that calves were being killed daily to fill their dinner plate. Most of the Greenpeace supporters are not truly aware of the vital part that the hunt plays in the lives of some Newfoundlanders.

I was very pleased and encouraged when this spring a large number of people turned out to see the sealers off in the old traditional way. The campaign by the local government hopefully will have some good effect. I think films concentrating on individual sealers and their families and way of life would force outsiders to look at the other side of the story.

When I wrote my poem I had hoped to make people think about the seal hunt as a way of life that has been going on for hundreds of years and to point out that the Newfoundland sealers were neither cruel nor unfeeling men who killed for greed or sport, but rather a breed of brave, hard-working, proud men and that to condemn them without any real thought as to their situation was to show one's own ignorance and lack of compassion for one's own fellow beings.

To my knowledge, no member of my family has ever been involved in the hunt, although we always had seal meat. I have watched and talked with many young sealers who were heading for the sealing ships (many for the first time), and although I was young myself at the time, I remember the admiration I had for these young men because most of them I felt were really frightened at the prospect of heading out to the fields but never was there any mention made of this by them, only that they had families who were depending upon the income they would receive at the end of the hunt. It is indeed a crime that these same men should now be labelled as cruel and heartless men . . .

Sincerely,
Elizabeth Sheardown

Mrs. Sheardown's letter elaborates on the sentiments expressed in her poem. She is obviously committed to the effort of restoring a good reputation to the Newfoundland people: her entry into the contest "for the opportunity to express my views from coast to coast," the phone call to the Greenpeace supporter, and sending copies of her poem to friends and family in Nova Scotia and Newfoundland, suggests that she perceives the issue as vital, and that she believes she may be able to communicate her case to the public. This objective is put forth at the end of her poem: "But I would be happy if I could help one person see/ That the Newfoundland sealers aren't cruel men/ Only do what they must for a living to win." This is repeated in her letter. ". . . I had hoped that someone would want to include my poem as material in an anti-Greenpeace protest."

The poem itself draws on the familiar arguments: tradition, economic necessity, and occupational hardship. The tone of the poem changes as it progresses; the first two stanzas are rather light and playful, but the transition is made through sobering images of "stormy March winds," "treacherous ice floes" and "foundered ships." Reproach is her tone for protesters who earn easy money through playing on the emotions of uncritical supporters.

Although Mrs. Sheardown claims no illusions about her role as a verse-maker: "Now a song writer I know I never will be," some of her comments suggest disappointment at the lack of recognition or appreciation from anyone outside her immediate friendship circle. The statement about the liability of a controversial topic for the radio poetry contest may have been her own personal way of preparing herself for disappointment.

Rex Hemeon, Botwood

(Untitled)

It's over for another year and the Greenpeace have gone
home
But I bet they'll be back next year cause they won't leave
us alone.
There'll be uncle Brian Davies and his hearty women crew
It's just too bad these people can't find better things
to do.

They say we're awfully cruel because we kill the seal,
I'd like to explain to them just how we Newfies feel.
We don't travel to the ice flows because it's so much fun,
It's just another way to have to increase our income.

My father, his father and grandfather before
They travelled to the ice flows for a hundred years or
more.
They left their families home for months to go and hunt
the seal
You have to be a Newfie to understand just how we feel.

We know they're things that happen in this world that are
more cruel,
Because we are Newfies don't mean we are fools.
How about the children that starve in other lands,
Let's think about the golden rule and help our fellow man.

We realize the need to conserve the things God gave to us
We got so many years without demonstration and such fuss.
The whole world's guilty of neglect, yes every single man,
So let your conscience be your guide before you judge our
Newfoundland

Now we always have a welcome for anyone on earth
To come and spend some time with us and see just what
we're worth.
You'll find our doors are open and our friendship is for
real.
We're not cruel the way some think just because we kill
the seal.[24]

I was unable to locate Rex Hemeon and cannot provide any biographical data and information about previous verse-making experience. The poem was probably written in 1976 after Brian Davies' visit with his "hearty women crew."

Economic necessity and tradition are the justifications for the hunt. Hemeon is concerned to answer the charges of ecological irresponsibility and cruelty. Further, he is concerned with restoring a positive image to Newfoundlanders. Through gentle reproach, the protesters are requested to be more reasonable and devote their energies to more demanding problems.

John White, Cormack

The Greenpeace Mission

In the year Nineteen Hundred Seventy Five
The planning of the Greenpeace hit our news,
The killing of the Seal, they would appeal,
They were coming to Newfoundland
To take a determined stand,
And with green dye, mark all the baby seals.

The Greenpeace group did reach St. Anthony,
Where the Northern Ice flows, and the Seals pass by,
Not coaxed along, by no Pacific tide,
They were met there, by men of Iron will,
In the season of the Kill,
And the misinformed soon recognized their pride.

Cause its just another crop,
That fishermen must harvest,
If the Fisherman must take a living from the sea,
Its not for the cruelty, or the blood,
That a Sealer kills a Seal Pup,
He's as Human, as others, pretend to be.

Its a Harvest that gives Dollars
To many Fishermen of this Island,
Their fathers, and Forefathers before that,
Its true, our Island has paid the price,
For the Seal-Hunt at the Ice,
In hardship, and loss of Life,
Our Island has paid for every ounce of fat.

But our Sealer, is a hard-working reaper,
And if there is blood on his hands,
Its part of his Livelihood, way of life,
He don't feel no guilt, nor shame,
As a few, big City Snobs, may claim,
To Him its honest bread, forgetting strife.

All our Experts say the Seal Fishery,
Is in no danger, becoming Extinct,
So what was the Greenpeace commotion, all about.
Was it for Publicity that they were gunning,
To keep the Donations incoming,
That gives easy Bread and Butter, no doubt.

Yet there are so many Avenues,
Where the blood of life flows free,
And the good Angels of Mercy never tread,
As the slaughtering is hidden,
And Intruders are forbidden,
To Photograph and show the world, the Dead.

Yet they show the bloody movies,
Of the Newfoundland Seal Hunt,
And try to tell the World, of a Barbaric Man,
There's no justice, except in truth,
Call him not, a cold-blooded brute,
He appreciates being called a Fisherman.

There are Ladies, so they say,
Who could not wear fur of seal,
It would keep reminding them of cruelty,
Let the beautiful mink coat be the rage,
Do they think the mink die of old age,
And donate their hides, to Society.

When Conservation be the motto,
Such Group's deserve a lot of praise,
But if its Hate of Killing, and love only for baby seals
Then they should get their Angles straighter,
As the Master of a freighter,
Now that they know, just how the Newfie Sealer feels.[25]

John White died in 1976 at the age of 59. His widow replied to my letter and said her husband had composed topical verses since the early 1940s, with newspapers often providing inspirational ideas. He wrote primarily for his own personal satisfaction, but he often shared his work with family and friends. The Whites knew men who had gone to the ice, but no one in their immediate family were sealers.

The poem begins as a narrative--the scene, actors, and the action are identified--but it quickly becomes a lengthy counter-protest expression. The familiar justifications are presented, with repeated appeals for the fisherman's cause. The extinction theory is denied: "All our Experts say the Seal Fishery/ Is in no danger, becoming Extinct/ So what was the Greenpeace commotion all about?" The protest films are cited as injurious, and the ignoring of slaughterhouses as unfair. Ladies wearing mink are made to feel guilty. The author ends on a very strong note, again appealing to reason: he praises conservation efforts but points out that they are misdirected in the sealing controversy.

Philomena Doran, St. John's

The Seal Hunt: "Let it be!"

Yahweh created all living things,
Both on the land and in the sea;
He made them to support us humans,
He said, "let it be, let it be."

He looked and said, "it would be good"
Fish, plants, animals in galore,
That we may have a livelihood;
Now, could we ask for more.

Saves from the flood, in Noah's Ark,
Those creatures of other times,
Imprints as seen an ancient walls,
Show unbroken ancestral lines.

Such a beautiful creation for rich and poor,
Ermine, crocodile so fine in clothes,
Reindeer and seals in the frozen north,
Which keep the life in the Eskimos.

Now with the seals we are concerned,
Rich in fat, food, furs, a prize;
Some folks are enchanted
With their big and doleful eyes.

A sealer was my great-grandfather,
His ship was all aglow,
As he sailed for the icefloes on her,
Over one hundred years ago.

For all the seals that he did take,
'T was said to be his due,
And a silken flag was given,
To Captain George Carew.

The seal hunt has been with us,
Since Cabot sailed the Main,
Brian Davies is trying to stop it,
Our heritage to disclaim.

He tried to discredit us,
To the naive he does appeal;
He only cares about himself,
And not about the seal.

For the show comes Bridget Bardot,
Boys! oh what a doll,
To try and stop the seal hunt,
She had an awful gall.

She gives of her wealth for animals,
She's made herself our foe,
To deny human beings a living,
For shame on you Bardot!

Our sealers have been hounded,
Oh, will they never ceased
By people who use meat and fur,
And call themselves Greenpeace.

What would we ever do,
Without the sealers brave and true,
Who face danger their families to enhance,
And keep the seals within balance.

Now, says Frankie baby,
A job it must be done,
I'll show 'em Newfoundlanders,
Are not too green to burn.

I'll cross the briny ocean,
And then I will demand
They stop their interfering
In the affairs of Newfoundland.

People of American, Europe and Japan,
It is my obligation to expose to sham,
Seals are taken by other nations, thus
Why do you come and pick on us?

You say we are barbarians,
You treat us like the Huns;
We are a loving, gentle people,
We use sticks instead 'a guns.

Now for our fate and honor,
Don't listen to any lies,
Then if you come and visit us
We'll feed you flipper pies.

For the cause of the sealers,
'T was worth the time and the money
To make the trip to expose the fraud,
For meddling in our country's economy.

To Premier Moores and the crew,
A big Thank You is due.[26]

Philomena Doran is a native of St. Mary's Bay. She has always enjoyed poetry, but only recently has begun to write her own verses. Controversial subjects interest her, and she has had one previous poem published in the Evening Telegram. Her familiarity with sealing came from her mother's first cousin who was a survivor of the 1914 "Newfoundland" disaster,[27] and as noted in the poem, her great-grandfather was Captain George Carew, a respected sealing skipper. Mrs. Doran believes the protesters are not sincere in their concern for the seals, and she is angered by their ability to raise large sums of money at the expense of Newfoundlanders.

Her poem argues through sympathetic appeal for "the sealers brave and true." She claims the hunt has legitimacy on the basis of tradition: "Since Cabot sailed the Main"; of economic need, occupational hazard, and ecological responsibility: "Who face danger their families to enhance/ And keep the seals in balance"; and divine sanction: "Yahweh created all living things/ . . . He made them to support us humans." She reproaches Brian Davies, Bardot, and Greenpeace for disrupting a traditional activity, and praises Premier Frank Moores who led the international counter-campaign. Mrs. Doran refutes the charges of cruelty: "We are a loving, gentle people/We use sticks instead of guns."

POETS AND PERFORMERS, OR, THE RECOGNIZED AMATEURS

These verse-makers acknowledge their special status. They have received recognition through limited publication and public performance and seem to enjoy the opportunity to participate in local affairs. Some of them are occasionally asked to write a verse for a specific purpose, but generally their work is inspired by an event or an emotion.

Mary MacIsaac, Curling

Swilin' '77

The ice moved down in '77
As in countless years before.
With it came storms and hardship,
For the sealers leaving shore.
The harvest might be scanty,
Or it might be bountiful,
But the money earned by honest sweat
Is better than the dole

They couldn't go out fishing
With the ice jammed tight on land,
But there was meat aplenty,
With the seal pups right at hand,
And in their long tradition,
They walked out on heaving ice,
To bring in the March harvest,
That is part of northern life.

They knew the rules for killing,
As laid down by our country,
It was not in their nature
To adhere to cruelty;
But they came face to face with foes
That differed with their stand,
Who tried to stop our sealers,
And keep them on the land.

Degrading us, the Charlatans came,
With pockets lined with gold.
They came to save the "baby seals"
In copters, and so bold.
They pushed around our labouring men
Ignoring their invasion.
That angry Newfoundlanders rose
To voice their indignation.

The strangers got protection,
From our province-paid policemen.
Our men lay prostrate on the snow,
Aggressors walked on them.
Our spiritual leaders spoke for peace,
And for civility . . .
But policemen held the sealers down,
As the copters were set free.

Descendents from the July Drive,
And Vimy Ridge were there,
Who spurned the British insults,
That were hurled from London Square,
The slander from the poison pen,
Of Davies and his likes,
Had branded Newfoundlanders,
And impared their natural rights.

Now we have "human babes" to feed,
In the isle of Newfoundland,
This might be hard for slickers,
From outside to understand,
We have the elements to fight,
To earn the daily pay,
While parasites and hypocrites,
Take our good name away.

Don't come back Brian Davies,
With your ill-begotten goods,
And Green Peace folk,
Don't foul our shores,
Stay in your neck of woods.
You can't expect a welcome,
From the people that you've bled--
Tis time you stopped your begging
And took "stock" of your head.[28]

Mary MacIsaac has been writing verses since childhood, ". . . when I caught the fever from my father and others who wrote verses on any unusual happening." Nearly seventy now, she describes her verse-making impulse: ". . . like Paddy with a belly-ache--I'm all in spurts. There are some things that only a poem or song can justify!" Mary taught elementary-school children for many years, and put her talent to use writing personalized poems for her students (the collection was published as Newfie Rhymes). Though she has no illusions about the literary merit of most of her work, she enjoys writing, and sometimes thinks it pleases others.

The MacIsaac family has been interested in traditional culture for many years, particularly in Scottish dancing and music as played in the Codroy Valley. The family performs at festivals and concerts around the province.

Part of her letter is reprinted below:

I'm very touchy about rights--and I just saw red. I sent my poem to Richard Cashin--and heard from him some months later! Had it published in the Humber Log (our weekly), and it went over well . . .

No one encouraged me to write "Swilin' '77," that's one thing you don't get here--you've just got to take the bull by the horns yourself--even if you are a woman! I have had a lot of requests for this poem, and had duplicates made in order to satisfy. I sent one to the Toronto Star! I'm a bit shy about treking my work--perhaps a bit cowardly--in my home they sort of think it is a joke.

My great grandfather in the Codroy Valley was a successful seal hunter, captaining his own ship in the 1880s in the Gulf fishery. Later my grandfather on both sides of the family pursued the hunt in the Gulf of St. Lawrence. My father made his first and last voyage at the age of 19; he did not like clubbing the pup seals, but it was the custom to go to the fishery to prove your manhood.

My Scottish grandfather, John Gillis, described to his grandchildren, over and over again, the beauty of the sunrise on Easter Sunday morning and on the Gulf icefield. It was a phenomena of dancing light. Although we youngsters got up early every Easter morn to see the sun dance, we were always disappointed.

The last seal caught in my family was in the 1920s when my brother, Wallace Gillis, killed a seal in the Codroy Harbour and pulled it ashore--over the ice--with a string attached to the tail. He was exhausted when he landed ashore and no wonder--all the old timers had a great time teasing him in going against nature in hauling a seal against the grain--you know it wouldn't slip along the way he had it rigged up . . . .[29]

Mrs. MacIsaac thinks the protesters are involved only because it is a lucrative business. "The protesters will get weaker as the voice of truth gets stronger. Frank Moores and others did a good job." She believes that Newfoundlanders should defend the hunt, for "as stood our fathers, so should we."

"Swilin' '77" is a strong and emphatic statement to protesters and Newfoundlanders alike. In some respects, it is a call for unity and determination to protect a traditional activity from external disturbance. The British, who participated in the protest, are chided with recollections of the fighting Newfoundlanders who gallantly gave their lives for the sake of their freedom. Partially a narrative, the poem documents some of the events of the 1977 protest. It is a poem of praise for the sealers and bitter accusations against the protesters. There is little doubt about her position: "Don't foul our shores/ Stay in your neck of woods/ You can't expect a welcome/ From the people that you've bled."

Angus Lane, Buchans

Green Peace or the Wearin' O' the Green

All ye who know of sealers brave attend both young and old
I feel it is my duty this story to unfold
About these Green Peace people their dastardly scheme
To have our little whitecoats awearin' o' the green.

That furry little creature with its coat of snowy white
To the sealers, hard-earned money as the elements they fight
Where's our M.P.'s?--Our Government? Why don't they intervene
To prevent our whitecoats from awearin' o' the green.

Let's drive them back across the Gulf--clear across the land
Ah yes me boys they'll rue the day they came to Newfoundland
We'll all know your colour then 'twill be yellow not bright green
They would not dare to have our seals awearin' o' the green

We have our muzzleloaders, the 12-gauge and the gaff
We can blast them all to kingdom come and then sit back and laugh
At their crazy antics as they scamper from the scene
Where they would have the little ones awearin' o' the green.

Man should not foul with nature's way but let it take it's course
God's plans we should not tamper with nor should we doubt their source
Let's spray Brian Davies green--that's what he is 'twould seem.
Then we'd have a limey awearin' o' the green.[30]

Angus Lane is 56 years old. Born in Fortune Harbour, Notre Dame Bay, he worked as a weighmaster for twenty-one years, and prior to that, he worked as a warehouse checker. He has written verses since boyhood--mostly satirical--for personal satisfaction and for the amusement of his friends. Recently, Breakwater Books, Ltd., released a recording of his songs (Come Hell or High Water) written about the Buchans miners' strike.

Mr. Lane regards the protesters as unemployed, publicity-seeking individuals who are using the sealing issue as an easy way to earn money. The song reprinted here was written for a variety show presented in St. Theresa's Parish Hall on St. Patrick's Day, 1976. The formulaic opening, "All ye who know of sealers brave, attend both young and old," is an indication the song is intended for a sympathetic audience. "Our little whitecoats" suggests a sense of propriety which is repeated in the final stanza: "God's plans we should not tamper with nor should we doubt their source."

The retaliation threats, albeit facetious, imply that sealers take their work seriously and will not tolerate "foolishness" indefinitely. Normally, such threats would not be amusing, but in this context the satire is immediately discernible. By reversing the protesters' plans, (spraying them with the dye intended for the seals) the author speaks for Newfoundlanders in the expression of hostility.

Michael Butler, St. John's

One Sealing Ship from Newfoundland (1975)

In former years great fleets of ships
To the icefields used to go
Job Brothers and the Bowring firms
Adventurous spirit did show
Great ships like Beothic, the Neptune and Kyle
Each spring to the ice, they'd be there in good style.

The Bloodhound and the Southern Cross
The Viking, Labrador
The Eagle and the Algerine
The Newfoundland and more
Great ships such as these were the pride of our Isle
Each spring to the ice, they'd be there in good style.

But now today from Newfoundland
To the icefield just one ship
Her destination is the Front
Perhaps she'll make one trip.
A shame does it seem with the seals round our coast
That only one ship can hunt seals at the most.

The merchants now have lost the drive
Their former traders had
When the pioneering spirit lived
In years when times were bad
No risks they will venture or small quotas take
Less paying returns on their seal hunt they make.

With meat and fish so dear to buy
It seems an idea good
To send more ships out to the ice
And process seals for food
With Newfoundland so near to the seals when they come
It seems just a shame that we only take some.

If other nations kill our seals
Why not our ships the same?
Why let Norwegians fill their ships?
Where is our pride and shame?
They have to cross Oceans, great outfits to buy,
Yet we near the harvest, let our seal fishery die.

The Greenpiece [sic] Intrusion (1976)

The Greenpiece crowd, we say to you
Before it is too late
Don't come out here to Newfoundland
To stop our sealing date
Don't try to stop our fishermen
From killing seals they need
To make a living from the sea;
To warning such pay heed.

Few sealing ships are now engaged,
So sealing herds have grown
Not like in former days of hunt
When fabulous kills were known.
The seals must be in millions now
Off the Funks and to the South
When ships so few go out to kill
So why do Greenpiece pout.

You have no business to come here
The seals are not your own
So keep your green dye to yourselves
And wisely stay at home
Our fishermen will watch for you
Don't let them see your dye
For if they catch you using it
You may's well say: "GOOD BYE."

We hope the Federal Government
Will enforce its regulations
To stop this interference
By the Greenpiece Dye Foundation
Those busy bodies we don't want
And neither do the seals
So stay at home you Greenpiece gripes,
Keep off from our icefields.

Leave Us in Peace (1977)

Boo, boo to you Franz Weber,
Brian Davies and Greenpeace
Go back from where you came from last,
And let us live in peace.

Who wants your presence here
You interfering crowd
"Go home and never come back again"
We warn you good and loud.

We're really come to something
To something that is new
When foreigners must come in here
And tell us what to do.

And give the seals a human cult,
A worship all their own,
A foolish sense of worship trait,
With extreme overtone.

What arrogance and dastard face,
To come a second year,
To try displace an industry,
Our fishermen hold so dear!

For sealing is our way of life
How dare you interfere!
From animals killed you get your meat
And fur on the coat you wear.

No one from here goes to your land
To interfere with you
He would be fined or put in jail
And be told just what to do.

But you so bare-faced and so bold
Come here for confrontation;
Cause trouble, and incite our men
By your senseless provocation.

Our sealing hunt is lawful,
Conservation we uphold;
We kill seals the most humane way,
Not what the films told.

So Weber and the Greenpeace crowd,
Brian Davies and his crew;
Your time engage for better use
Find better things to do.

Stay home and fight abortion
Injustices and crime
Try fighting hunger for the poor
Then for seals no fighting time.

Send-Off for Our Sealers (1978)

Despite the cold and blustery day
It didn't keep the crowds away
From Dockside St. John's, 'twas suffice
Four ships were leaving for the ice.
A good send off with hearty cheer
Prefaced by service, band and prayer
The clergymen were there with grace
As the blessing of the ships took place
Hal Andrews chairman's job did lend
Saw program fulfilled to the end
It seemed tradition born anew
With the public cheers for ships and crew
With rousing animation grand
'Twas a glorious day for Newfoundland.

The TV crews and camera men
Were backing ships and crews we send
Recording for the world to see
The importance of our seal industry
And while proceedings went with pride
The "Norma Gladys" she did glide
Across the harbor gracefully
To make sure things went smoothly
Back on the wharf while thousands cheered
A protestor Elliot did appear
He got into a fighting spree
And was taken into custody
The police were quick with sturdy hand
To make protestors understand
Their stunts to stop our men did fail
And soon they'd land themselves in jail.
And Captain Johnson spoke so plain
And proudly thanked the crowds who came
He knew the people's hearts were true
For wishing well their ships and crew.

The captain really felt enticed
To be going again out to the ice
And Premier Moores in parka red
Stood on the platform bare of head
While strong wind blew and snow whizzed by
He wished the sealers, Luck, Good Bye.
While bells did ring and whistles blared
The ships out through the Narrows steered.[31]

from "So Many Snags for Newfoundland" (1978)

. . . And now our Newfoundlanders have to fight
to hunt our seals
They are snagged by opposition by the
Greenpeace howls and squeals;

They are snagged by Brian Davies who has
joined with one to strive,
Who claims he killed 12,000 seals and
skinned the pups alive.[32]

Michael Butler was born "shortly after the first World War" in Bristol's Hope, Conception Bay. He is retired from a career in teaching. He writes "to express my views; to see them in print (not too proud); to create enjoyment; to keep my mind at work and not let it become rusty; to bear witness to God and to my country; to be of some help in adding to our Newfoundland songs and tradition; it's a great pastime when indoors; and finally, I LIKE DOING IT."

Mr. Butler writes about all subjects that interest him: "war, nature, outer space, politics, religion, Remembrance Day, peace, vandalism, abortion, education, Christian Brothers, tributes, entertainment, Christmas, Lower Churchill, Quebec, etc." He frequently submits letters-to-the-editor with poems to accompany his thoughts. Three archives, at the Newfoundland Historical Society, the St. John's Public Library and the library at the Newfoundland Teachers' Association, have files of his work. His verses have been published in the Newfoundland Teacher's Association journals, the Newfoundland Quarterly and in other local journals.

Mr. Butler's acquaintance with Cecil Mouland, one of the survivors of the 1914 "Newfoundland" disaster, may account for the author's interest in the seal fishery. "I wrote those verses about the seal protesters to strengthen and support Newfoundland's stand in its defense--of the seal hunt, and for the enjoyment I get in knowing I have helped. If my verses activated others to participate in anti-protest activity in any form (apart from violence or illegal kind), so much the better, but I hardly know that. Perhaps they were not taken that seriously."

A chronological analysis of Mr. Butler's sealing verses is useful because it demonstrates how his attitude changes. The verse written in 1975 laments the passing of a tradition and suggests that apathy--on the part of merchants and the government--is responsible for the decline of the seal fishery. He uses his verses to communicate his own personal values, with emphasis on integrity, courage, and duty towards history and tradition. "One Sealing Ship from Newfoundland" utilizes a familiar feature of folksong in that it presents a catalogue of famous sealing ships, lest the public forget the past. It is a protest expression in that it describes and criticizes a contemporary problem, but it lacks the indignation and argumentation of the 1976-78 verses.

In "The Greenpiece Intrusion" (1976), the protesters are mocked--"Greenpiece Dye Foundation"--and Newfoundland's right to pursue the hunt is asserted. The rhetoric is unmistakable--"our" icefields and Greenpiece "gripes" suggest the author views the conflict as unjust and irresponsible.

By 1977, Michael Butler's attitude towards interference by outsiders was indignant and incredulous. "Leave us in Peace" documents the principal actors of the protest (Weber, Davies, and Greenpeace--by now he has corrected his spelling), and is derivative of a speech made by Richard Cashin, who suggested that seal-worship was becoming a new cult. This poem is the most emotional of his series on sealing and possibly is the most spontaneous, defiant outburst of frustration and anger that the author could allow himself to make.

The following year, on 5 March, Newfoundlanders rallied to demonstrate their support behind the sealers; "Send-Off for Our Sealers," a narrative account of the events of the day, celebrates the unity of Newfoundlanders and their determination to revive a faltering custom. Mr. Butler is obviously pleased with this renewed public spirit and the poem conveys this sense of approval.

But later in the spring of the same year, Mr. Butler submitted a poem to the Evening Telegram entitled, "So Many Snags for Newfoundland." It is a lament for all the ill-fated projects and economic disappointments experienced by the province. Yet his determination to overcome the obstacles is evident. "But fight, we will, we won't give in, our future is at stake . . ." The sixth stanza reprinted above, rebukes the Newfoundlander who turned against his homeland to work with Brian Davies (Ray Elliott). The tone is resigned and somewhat bitter--the anger of some of his earlier verses has dissipated.

PROFESSIONAL PERFORMERS

Ron MacEachern, Pat Sulley and Gary O'Driscoll are professional performers, often remunerated for their music. Their experience and public exposure vary considerably. Ron MacEachern, a Nova Scotian, has become a well-known folksong performer in the Atlantic provinces and has made appearances on national radio and television programs; Pat Sulley is a St. John's musician, who occasionally performs in other communities; Gary O'Driscoll appeared at the 2nd Annual Folk Arts Festival in St. John's in 1978.

Ron MacEachern, Sydney, Nova Scotia

Newfoundland Sealers (<u>ca</u>. 1977)

chorus: Oh ye Newfoundland sealers all hands be behind ye
you're the salt of the earth each and every man,
all hands for Newfoundland's right in the fishery
Davies be gone for you're less than a man.

Now I shall not be long with the words I would tell you
let our island be rid of this Green Peacer band
there's not one man nor woman should stand for
their treachery
all hands for Newfoundland sealers will stand.

(chorus)

And our children will go as their fathers before them
our men who have toiled and our men who have died
will not be put under by the filth of the Greenpeace
our rights and our island will not be denied.

(chorus)

--tune: "The Ryans and the Pittmans," or,
"We'll Rant and We'll Roar."

Untitled (<u>ca</u>. 1977)

Oh me boys they are the sealers
no they're not the money stealers
like the companies that control the Greenpeace dollars
them that preaches and that teaches
still they always come like leaches
for our fish and for our seal when hunger hollers.

chorus: Send me pogy way of Logy Bay
for on this Rock I mean to stay
I'm telling you this my dear so I will save ye
the trouble and the commotion
of coming across the little ocean
with that lyin' gutless thieving Brian Davies

yes me boys they are the sealers
no they wouldn't be the stealers
makes our living from the sea its very proper
and sure from here to Harbour Grace
there's not one man'll disgrace this place
like the likes of a Royal Canadian Mounted Copper.

(chorus)

And you boys up in Toronto
where you get the jobs so pronto
working in factories working in canneries makin' deals
either your canneries going to shut down
or the staff in half will cut down
when me boys refuse to go for fish and seal.

(chorus)

It was while he was a student at Memorial University that Ron MacEachern became sympathetic to the sealing issue. "I wrote both songs in about a week after I got a call from Chris Brooks who said he wanted me to play with the Mummers' anti-Greenpeace show . . . I knew that I would be able to sing and bring attention to the other side of the issue."

Ron adapted both songs to tunes already familiar to Newfoundlanders: "Off to Philadelphia," and "My Name is Mrs. Nevilles and I'm from the Higher Levels." The message he conveys is one of support with references to tradition, the fishery, and self-sufficiency. The emotionalism that colours the words of the other poets is missing, perhaps because he recognizes his role as a performer who acts as a catalyst for action, rather than as an agent.[33]

Pat Sulley, St. John's

Coffee on the Last Day (ca. 1978)

Have one more cup of coffee she said before you go
Oh no, I must be leaving now, to brave the truly cold.
There's a ship out in the harbour and its ready for to go
To hunt the seal to make a meal to keep my woman warm.

I love your face I love your hands I love to watch you work
I love your fresh hot-buttered bread the way you hang your
skirt.
Get out she said and don't come back and hung on to my shirt.
You're a brazen lad and I love you mad, don't leave me sad
and hurt.
You know it must be cold out there when Shelagh's Brush
is on
When March steps in your back is bared and bodies do get
numb.
That sailors who go sailing must sail until they're done
On the icy fields where life is real and nature hides
her guns.

And when I think of frozen ice it chills me to the bone.
I think of you and what I'd do if you did not come home.
You shouldn't think of me like that, I'm strong and still
I'm young.
I love you true, your eyes of blue, your body safe and
young.

The bells are ringing in the town, the anchor's being
weighed
From ladies on the dock no sound, the schooner leaves
the bay
Into the wind-swept ocean to prairies cold and grey
To the frozen fields where life is real and winter's made
to pay.[34]

Pat Sulley began writing this song in 1977, but as he explained, "I had to leave it for awhile to arrive at a more objective, less emotional song." The song is based on a hypothetical situation--the setting is the turn of the century and the actors are newlyweds. Neither the bride nor her husband want to be apart but both know it is necessary if they are to survive the winter.

Although this is not a counter-protest song, its composition was stimulated by the renewed public interest in sealing. Pat Sulley is convinced that the protesters, and Greenpeace in particular, are using the seal hunt for their own financial gain. "Coffee on the Last Day" is an effort to depict an emotional situation, a scene which undoubtedly was repeated many times over when sealing was a major industry. The recreation of a tender moment between a man and a woman makes its appeal universal.

There are interesting parallels in this poem to Solomon Samson's poem, "A Sealer's reply to his Wife,"[35] although a note suggests the characters are grandparents instead of newlyweds. "So Maggie my darling/ I must leave you alone," is the husband's way of comforting his wife, promising, "And when we return/ With a good bumper trip/ You will soon forget/ That I gave you the slip." The difference in rhetorical strategy is that Sulley's hero is not really anxious to go to the ice, but economic necessity is implied as the cause for his leaving. Maggie's more mature husband is responding to "The call of the ice-fields, [which] makes me feel restless/ At this time of year." Both verses belong to the sympathetic/ reproach category, although the opposition is nature and potential hazards rather than protesters.

Gary O'Driscoll, Bay Bulls

A Sealing Song (ca. 1978)

Early in the month of March the sealing is beginning
While back there in the abattoirs the butchers they are skinning
Baby lambs and baby hams to clothe and feed the nations.
While sealers brave the elements to reach their destination.

Johnson in his Lady ship sails on the north Atlantic
He keeps his head to all that's said despite the protest frantic
Davies and that Greenpeace bunch are screaming with emotion
While simple men are labouring out on the frozen ocean.

Living in the stormy white all in the dead of winter
Slaving in this bloody hell the papers call adventure
Facing death with every step to feed his wife and family
Loving not the deed he does nor does he find it manly.

Actresses and Congressmen come in the fair blue morning
Caring not for man or seal, publicity they're yearning
Cowhide gloves and moneyed belts caress the tearless whitecoat
Each year this plastic pantomime is enacted on the ice
floes.

The protest is big business now, yes bigger than the sealing
To people all around the world for money they're appealing
With falsities and pictures and emotions they're deceiving
From people who are blinded untold billions they're
receiving

Now to conclude and finish, of my people I will tell
A thousand men have frozen still out on the Arctic hell
Some say they are barbarians, our dignity they slander
While I am proud to tell you, I'm a native Newfoundlander.[36]

Gary O'Driscoll is a recent Memorial University graduate who hopes to pursue a career in real estate. He does not perform regularly, but occasionally sings at special events such as conventions, the St. John's Folk Club, and festivals. He wrote "A Sealing Song" in 1978 because he heard so many people "getting upset and angry, and at the time, I was getting upset in the same way, and so, rather than be arguing all the time, I just wrote a song about it."

The song is sung as a lament, with stress given to the hardships of a sealer's life. The protesters are reproached for wearing "cowhide gloves and moneyed belts," appealing with "falsities and pictures," and receiving "untold billions" from people around the world. In the sense that the song praises simple men (". . . slaving in the bloody hell the papers call adventure/ facing death with every step to feed (his) wife and family"), it belongs to the celebratory/condemning rhetorical category. It is the first song to suggest "the protest is big business now, yes bigger than the sealing." It can be assumed to have been written in 1978 because it refers to the presence of the two U.S. Congressmen (Jeffords and Ryan), who witnessed the hunt at the invitation of the Greenpeace Foundation in that year.

A true counter-protest song, each verse contains an argument or counter-argument: (1) the reference to abattoirs is an oblique rebuttal to charges of cruel slaughtering of seal pups; (2) the contrast between protesters "screaming with emotion" while sealers labour "out on the frozen ocean" is sharply drawn; "Johnson" is Captain Morrissey Johnson, skipper of the "Lady Johnson II"; (3) the charge of sadism levelled against sealers is denied: "loving not the deed he does nor does he find it manly"; (4) the popularized image of the whitecoat pup "crying" is corrected with the phrase "tearless whitecoat"; (5) the protesters are charged with the use of false propaganda for financial profit, while Newfoundlanders (verse 6) are praised for their valour and dignity. The author is ". . . proud to tell you, I'm a native Newfoundlander."

PUBLIC VOICES

Nish Collins, Art Scammell, John Crosbie, and Miller Ayre are familiar names in the local media. They are recognized 'voices' of the people, whose energies and careers are dedicated to preserving and supporting the interests of Newfoundlanders. They are articulate, self-conscious spokesmen of a large, but often anonymous, constituency. Arguing from a common rhetorical base, their verses are truly cultural statements that transcend social boundaries and are meaningful to many.

Nish Collins, St. John's

Trial and Error

One Brian Davies, meddler,
Has had his case postponed
In May continued hearings
A thing we have bemoaned.

The sealers will be gone then
To places far and wide
For men whose work is seasonal
Are quite diversified.

If it's held in Toronto
Then there is no fair play
For there his sympathizers are
Opinions they will sway.

Bert Davies and Greenpeacers
Deserve a big salute
Aimed at each one's posterior
With steel toed safety boot.[37]

Untitled

Imagine Walter Carter asking natives
Not to harass Brian Davies, utter rot
Whatever we think government is doing
It's more than obvious what it is not.

Hello protect Brian Davies and Greenpeacers!
If anything give it much more clout
The government should serve on them injunction
And drive him and the bloody works straight out.

The riot act was read to the wrong people
St. Anthony should not be the scene of stress
But leaders through ineptness and inaction
Have put our people in this sorry mess.

Disgraceful is the word, you throw injunctions
At people on the pickets, now get smart
Let charity at home begin, great leaders
And get rid of the Englishman upstart.[38]

Our Lips are Sealed

A little late for Premier Moores
to make his overture
When horse is stolen it's too late
to lock the stable door
The damage is already done
by Davies and Greenpeace
Bardot acted out her part
"zees cruelty" to cease.

That was the time for Premier Moores
his office to assert
It's much too late, the damage done,
our seal hunt has been hurt.
Protesters should have been denied
the access to the Front
Instead of curtesies to them
we should have been more blunt.

Greenpeace, Weber, anti-hunt
proponents got for free
A coverage quite ill-deserved
through our stupidity
In letting them advance so far,
what they said wasn't true
A challenge to the media [39]
let's see what you can do.

Mammals and Men

This Brian Davies, Who is he?
Who makes waves of publicity
And pitch emotional employs
To make a multi-nation noise
Face value the remarks he made
With manner confident displayed
Revealing questions none did ask
Of any background for his task
In what did Davies graduate
Why to seals did he gravitate
Could he have attained his degree
From synthetic fur industry
A mammal can't equate with man
A life state there's no higher than
What's all this talk of "baby seal"
When making a tear jerk appeal
A "pup" is this young mammal's due
Then why creation misconstrue
All form of growth, life-land and sea
Were made, then man, crowning glory
The other forms of things alive
Designed to help humans survive
Through slick promotion harm was done
Big question, is there anyone
Who can dig up the Davies deal [40]
That makes him expert on the seal.

Nish Collins is a regular columnist for the St. John's Daily News, writing the "Rhymes of the Times" column since 1971. When I asked him what he thought his rhymes accomplished, he replied: ". . . communication. Somewhere along the route I hope to touch all my readers. Through the conciseness of my writings, I feel I can emphasize a certain topic." Although Mr. Collins claims to have no favourite writers, he recalls reading Edgar A. Guest as a boy. "I do not model my writings after anyone. The spontaneity of my writings makes them original."

His "Rhymes" are topical, usually commenting on local issues. Some are political, while others are of a more reflective, personal nature. Highly esoteric, appreciation of Collins' "Rhymes" requires a familiarity with local personalities and events. In a sense, they are editorials in verse format.

"Trial and Error," refers to Brian Davies' arrest and the subsequent postponement of his trial in 1976. The next verse is much more indignant, and accuses the Provincial Fisheries Minister, Walter Carter, of betraying Newfoundlanders by warning them to abandon their protest at the Viking Motel in St. Anthony. "Our Lips are Sealed" refers to Premier Moores' pro-hunt publicity tour abroad in early 1978. A lot of money was spent getting the "facts" across and many Newfoundlanders were skeptical about the effort. The government had been slow to enter the controversy in previous years, and the blitz media campaign of 1978 was perceived by some as a politically-motivated scheme. The media's role in giving coverage to the protesters was another area of frequent criticism, and many observers believed the issue would have faltered several years earlier had the press refused to participate.

"Mammals and Men" is more specific in its appeal. Through pointed questions--"This Brian Davies, Who is He?"--Collins argues with the familiar rhetoric of counter-protest. Davies is satirized as a zealot without authority, and the seal hunt is justified by reasoning that ". . . man, crowning glory/ The other forms of things alive/ Designed to help humans survive." It is the only verse in this collection which cites divine sanction as the ultimate justification for the hunt.

John Crosbie, St. John's

(Untitled)

We got your message on the seals,
From whom we get some fur and meals;

You ask us for a closed season
Without you giving cogent reason.
You say you hate to have seals die,
While pigs and horses in France expire,
While snails and geese and frogs and cattle
Every day die with the French death rattle!
And what about your tortured goose,
Force-fed until his liver's loose,
Ready for the foie gras boost!
Your tears for seals do not impress
Until French sins you do confess;
This offer should give you a thrill:
Abolish for a year the Frenchman's kill
Of horses, geese, frogs and the snail:
Of nuclear testing, stop that tale:
Preserve the grape, don't make the wine,
And we will leave the seals behind.
Now France should learn the ancient truth,
That tit for that is always couth.
You eat your snails and frog's legs dipper
But I will stick with rum and flipper.[41]

John Crosbie, Member of Parliament, St. John's (West), is a career politician, and writes verse occasionally to ". . . amuse myself, and the audience is usually just a few friends." With this satirical ode to Brigette Bardot, Mr. Crosbie's verse-making went public, and he provided the House of Commons and his Newfoundland constituency with a good laugh about a subject that has not been very amusing.

Although none of his close friends or immediate relatives were sealers, the Crosbie family owned the sealing vessels, "Sir John Crosbie" and "Chesley A. Crosbie." As a Newfoundlander who promotes industry, John Crosbie is concerned that the anti-hunt campaign will cause the decline of pelt prices and consequently hasten the closure of the fishery. He does not argue romantically and his reasoning is based on strict marketing principles.

In this poem, Brigette Bardot is the scapegoat for France's political stand regarding seal-pelt importation. This verse belongs to the celebratory/condemning category because it argues for fairness and justice through counter-accusation and defense. Yet as an amusement, composed somewhat whimsically, it may be classified as epideictic rhetoric.

Art Scammell, St. John's

A Sealer's Song

Come all you Newfoundlanders and listen to my song
About St. Anthony's visitors from "away" and "upalong";
There were movie types and media types and Mounties
some fivescore,
If we were bent on violence they'd need a hundred more.

They are out to ban the seal hunt and this they mean to do,
Brian Davies and the Greenpeacers and all their motley crew;
This year they've got Franz Weber with phony fur to sell-
A bleeding heart from Switzerland who thinks he's William Tell.

They say the seals are threatened but the evidence is clear,
With quotas carefully controlled, of that there is no fear;
We're the endangered species who live by coastal seas,
We kill the seal as we kill fish to feed our families.

A bedlamer boy from Greenpeace he chained on to the "whip,"
And was dunked into the water by the rolling of the ship;
We had a job to save him in all the fuss and racket,
But I bet his pelt wouldn't have been worth as much as a Ragged Jacket.

When Brigitte said in Paris she cuddled a whitecoat dear,
Sure every swiler in the land he grinned from ear to ear;
He knows from long experience she's pilin' on the lies,
A real whitecoat's talons would have slashed her face and eyes.

They call us cruel, barbaric, hunting seals just for the thrill--
These pampered city slickers that a day's hard work would kill;
What do they know of challenges of storm and sea and ice
That dare the blood to answer and to pay the sealers' price?

They're out for front-page stories, they've come so far to roam.
And blood on the ice will show up well on T.V. screens back home;
They know their media bosses have paid good money out
If they don't send "juicy" stories their jobs are "up the spout."

There's many things we don't approve in countries far away.
How people act and dress and talk and how they earn their pay;
But we don't get up a hate campaign and stir up children too,
To force our views on other folks as these do-gooders do.

Our governments must keep these types from off the whelping ice,
Or there'll be tragedies to tell--we're men, not frightened mice;
We merit more protection than a motion on the floor--
Where will you get your flippers when the seal hunt is no more?

We're not adverse to meeting up with a star from Hollywood,
We sure would like to rescue her from an angry old Dog Hood;
But the Arctic floes are not the place, Yvette, to use your wiles,
We're not spruced up for courtin' when we're out there peltin' swiles!

We have to take from nature whate'er the seasons bring,
We're fishermen in summer and swilers in the spring;
If you don't approve the seal hunt, you have a right to
say.
But when we go out on the ice, don't try to bar our way.

So here's a health to Romeo, who took the sealers' part,
He stood up to protesters, he has our cause at heart;
And raise your glass to Tommy Hughes who tells it like
he knows,
And don't forget Rick Cashin when you're culling friends
from foes.[42]

Born in Change Islands, Art Scammell is one of the most beloved song-writer-poets of Newfoundland. He holds a B.A. degree from McGill University, an M.A. from the University of Vermont, and an honourary Doctor of Laws from Memorial University. R. M. Mowbray, University Orator, said of the candidate at the Spring, 1977, convocation: ". . . here is a bard, a poet and writer, a teacher; a livyer whose devotion to Newfoundland has been tempered by living away for awhile."[43] Mr. Scammell taught in Montreal for thirty years before returning home in 1970. His most popular song, "The Squid-Jiggin' Ground," has the distinction of being considered by many as the unofficial anthem of Newfoundland.

"A Sealers' Song," like many protest songs, has been adapted to a familiar tune--in this case, the popular "Old Polina." The author draws on all three rhetorical strategies to convey his opinion about the sealing controversy. He celebrates swilers for their industriousness, and condemns the protesters as: ". . . city slickers that a day's hard work would kill." He cites Romeo LeBlanc, Richard Cashin and Tom Hughes as men worthy of praise for their outspoken support for Newfoundlanders, whereas the opposition is ridiculed as "bleeding hearts," "bedlamers," and "media types."

The tone of the song changes from stanza to stanza. It begins with the traditional "Come all you" opening--a method of inviting sympathetic attention to a narrative which is intended to be informative as well as pleasing. Some verses appeal for compassion from those who are unfairly critical: "There's many things we don't approve in countries far away/ . . . But we don't get up hate campaigns and stir up children too . . .," and again, "If you don't approve the seal hunt, you have a right to say/ But when we go out on that ice, don't try to bar our way." The argument of extinction is disputed; ". . . the evidence is clear/ With quotas carefully controlled, of that there is no fear." There is the plea for Newfoundlanders: "We're the endangered species who live by coastal seas."

Sarcastic references to starlets (Bardot and Mimieux) contribute humour to an otherwise serious subject. The media are reprimanded for their part in reporting only the sensational events to the exclusion of other relevant information. From an aesthetic viewpoint, "A Sealers' Song," is probably the best of the counter-protest collection, but Scammell's sentiments and rhetorical strategies parallel those of the other, less-skilled but equally motivated poets. The poem is assured a place in protest history since it has already been reprinted in several collections devoted to sealing.

Miller Ayre, St. John's

The Codpeace Song

How can you be so cod-descending
The protest groups slander us with such seal
The cry that the harp is so helpless and lovely
Don't you know how the coddle is their favourite meal
On the surface they might look real cute and cuddly
But deep down underneath they're savage and cruel.
Oh the sea it is filled with the tears and sad stories
Heart-broken codfathers, codmothers, too.

Now little Tommy cod met sweet young Connie
How they loved to meet and go for a swim in the school
But a harp seal flippered out and he ate up little Connie
Now Tommy he drinks till he's loaded to the gills
Crying cod-almighty, life is so cruel . . .

So let's raise the codscience of all conservationists
You can't cut no conners cause cods in this too
So before you seal the fate of the codfish
Find out all the facts we're codding on you
Good for the halibuts oh save my soul
Cod guard thee Newfoundland[44]

(sung by Terry Reilly and Glen Tilley; aired on St. John's radio in March, 1979)

Miller Ayre is the coordinator of "Codpeace," an organization which sprouted in the fall of 1978, when Ayre and several colleagues began to make plans for a counter-protest. On January 26, 1979, Codpeace was officially 'unveiled' at a St. John's Rotary Club luncheon.

Although the plight of "Cuddles Cod" versus the likes of the vicious "Heinrich von Harp Seal," satirized the motives of anti-sealing protesters, the motivation for this kind of appeal developed from accumulated frustration and anger. Unlike the majority of counter-protest expressions included in this collection, Codpeace is not spontaneous or reflexive. Instead, it is an organized, deliberate, and somewhat sophisticated form of counter-protest which solicits support through the use of bumper-stickers, buttons, and billboards.

Codpeace is national news, but its constituency remains provincially-based. Intellectually, mainlanders might appreciate the mimicry, but the appeal is unlikely to be persuasive to them because the content is so highly localized and esoteric. Without familiarity with the events and personalities of previous protest seasons, Codpeace rhetoric is reduced to a multiplicity of meaningless puns.

Despite its lack of spontaneity, Codpeace is like other counter-protest expressions in that it produces reactionary literature and uses publicity tactics. For example, hunt protesters have frequently used helicopters to reach the ice floes to film or disrupt the sealers at their work, so Codpeace dramatized its position by landing a helicopter in Bannerman Park (St. John's) to make the following announcement:

> CODPEACE has captured the Great Seal of the United States from the U.S. Consulate Building in St. John's. The CODPEACE organization warned President Codder in a telegram to the White House that action against the Seal would be taken if the U.S. Congress did not rescind Resolution 142 deploring the Canadian Seal Hunt.
>
> Since the U.S. has a seal hunt of its own off its West Coast, CODPEACE demands in the name of International Justice that President Codder personally repudiate Resolution 142 before midnight, George Washington's Birthday, February 22/79. Further, in the spirit of good-will the President is asked to return the seal skin coat codfiscated by his customs' officers from a recent Canadian delegate to the U.S.
>
> If the President does not comply with the requests of CODPEACE, the Great Seal of the United States will spend the rest of its life juggling balls in a travelling circus somewhere on the East Coast of Canada.[45]
>
> In Cod We Trust

It is interesting to see how Codpeace parody and satire contrasts with the sobriety of the "Save Our Swilers" type of rhetoric which circulated in 1977 and 1978. Possibly the popular acceptance of Codpeace may well indicate a more confident attitude among Newfoundlanders, as reflected in the remark of PRO spokesman, Eli Bryant, in St. Anthony: "If only Brian Davies would come this year . . . now we're ready for him."[46]

QUESTIONNAIRE AND SUMMARY OF RESPONSES

1. Do you write verses about other subjects? Have you ever published any of your work?

Bonnah: yes; for twenty years; everything that interests me; unpublished.
Butler: yes (see letter, Chapter 3).
Casey: only 3, while I was sick for 6 months.
Collins: yes, on a daily basis, 'Rhymes of the Times,' for seven years.
Doran: yes, about subjects that interest me; one poem published in the Telegram.
Goobie: no; just interested in this topic.
Hiscock: yes, since the fifth grade; one published.
Lane: yes, since boyhood; mostly satire; published previously.
MacIsaac: yes, since childhood, on a variety of subjects; published.
March: yes, for eight years - history, 'stories I have heard,' unpublished.
Menchions: yes, for 35 years, about anything that appeals to me; unpublished previously - this was a 'protest to the protesters.'
Mercer: yes; since early teens; children's stories; published.
Sheardown: one other poem, on the occasion of the birth of my daughter; it was a good way to express my view from coast to coast (CBC Morning Side show).

2. Why do you compose verses?

Bonnah: personal satisfaction.
Butler: see letter, Chapter 3.
Casey: for something to do.
Doran: to express my views.
Goobie: personal satisfaction.
Hiscock: I work out my frustration on paper.
Lane: personal satisfaction and friends.
MacIsaac: there are some things only a poem can justify!
March: personal satisfaction.
Menchions: personal satisfaction.
Mercer: I see humour in most things . . . I am a dreamer.
Pitts: to express my opinions.
Sheardown: for family and friends.

3. What kinds of response to you receive about your verse-making?

Bonnah: no response outside my family.
Butler: friends complement me, some people call.
Casey: a number of people called after they heard my song on 'Here and Now.'
Doran: several people have called to say they agree with me.
Goobie: compliments on my skill as a verse-maker.
Hiscock: few people outside my family know about it; I received most of my recognition while still in high school.
Lane: yes, they like my satirical verses.
MacIsaac: good response from family, friends, and school children.
March: some have asked for copies and have said I have skill as a verse-maker.
Menchions: sometimes people ask for copies.
Mercer: my children's stories have been taped and played in British schools.
Pitts: published in the Newfoundland Herald with a small payment for the effort.
Sheardown: family compliments.

4. Do you know anyone who has been to the ice?

   Bonnah: brother, friends, and other relatives.
   Butler: acquainted with Cecil Mouland, survivor of the 1914 "Newfoundland" disaster.
   Casey: I was a landsman; several friends from Bonavista went on the ships.
   Doran: great-grandfather and mother's first cousin.
   Goobie: 3 springs personally and father went.
   Hiscock: no.
   Lane: no.
   MacIsaac: grandfather.
   March: no; after reading Death on the Ice, I felt sorry for seal hunters.
   Menchions: I did several years ago; my father and brother went as well.
   Mercer: no.
   Pitts: no.
   Sheardown: no.

5. Why do you think Greenpeace and Brian Davies have chosen to protest the hunt?

   Bonnah: protesters' concern for the seals, however misguided, is commendable. If monetary gain is the motive, the organizations should be attacked and disbanded. Protesters can accomplish awareness to the fact the seal must not be over-harvested.
   Butler: for their own cause--money-making.
   Casey: to fill their pockets.
   Doran: for money.
   Goobie: they could make plenty of money if they got the seal fishery closed and their own factories working imitation fur.
   Hiscock: mostly for themselves.
   Lane: as a means of making money.
   MacIsaac: the protest is lucrative.
   March: the majority are trying to gain public recognition.
   Menchions: they protest the hunt for personal gain; they can get a fat and easy living by their protesting.
   Mercer: it could be the beautiful soulful brown eyes of the whitecoat which touched their heart, or publicity, or money and profits.
   Pitts: money and profits.

6. How would you describe the protesters?

   Bonnah: protesters are concerned citizens of the world; misinformed and out of touch with the realities of the hunt.
   Casey: looking for easy money so they don't have to work.
   Doran: greedy.
   Goobie: stupid to try to stop Newfoundlanders from killing seals.
   Hiscock: sensationalists; they may have been taken in by others and know very little about what is really happening.
   Lane: unemployed--they don't want to work and are seeking publicity.
   MacIsaac: out for themselves.
   March: people looking for attention.
   Menchions: they are not really protesters.
   Mercer: I am shocked and disgusted with the way this infamy has grown all out of proportion.

7. Is the future of the seal hunt threatened by protesters?

   Bonnah: possibly; with over-population of the herds, the seal will become a nuisance to the fishery.

Butler: it depends upon the markets and federal restrictions.
Casey: not by the protesters, but the sealers may get fed up with being called murderers.
Collins: they have not influenced those who harvest seals for a livelihood, or those who seek adventure. They may have enough emotional support to affect the sealskin market.
Doran: no.
Goobie: no.
Hiscock: definitely threatened.
Lane: not at all.
Menchions: no, eventually people will see what these people are up to.
Mercer: (yes); it will be too late after the seal hunt is banned or if all the markets are closed.
Pitts: yes, they could close down the industry.
Sheardown: yes, because they play on the emotions of people like my friend who now regard the baby seal as something akin to the human baby.

8. What should Newfoundlanders do to defend the hunt.

Bonnah: fight propaganda with propaganda.
Butler: protesters and journalists should not be allowed to view the hunt.
Casey: do like I did; block them everywhere.
Doran: express their views.
Goobie: get more Newfies interested in it.
Hiscock: perhaps form groups and visit other countries and point out the cruelties that exist among them.
Lane: ignore the protesters.
MacIsaac: As stood our fathers so we stand.
March: Newfoundlanders should keep cameramen off the ice.
Menchions: encourage people to hunt seals and ignore the protesters.
Mercer: I don't know, short of throwing all the protesters in jail.
Sheardown: yes, I was encouraged when this spring (1978) a large number of people turned out to see the sealers off in the traditional way. I think films concentrating on sealers and their families and their way of life would force outsiders to look at the other side of the story.

9. Do you think Newfoundlanders are sufficiently concerned about the future of the seal hunt?

Bonnah: more than ever before, thanks to all the publicity.
Butler: yes, but self-defense won't change too many notions now conceived of by people who respect animal pups more than little babies.
Casey: no.
Collins: yes, the involvement of the government, the strong home support and the manner in which the provoked sealers have kept their composure are positive elements.
Doran: yes.
Goobie: greater efforts should be made.
Hiscock: yes, but we may be too late.
Lane: the government succeeded, in my opinion.
MacIsaac: greater efforts are needed; better boundary laws.
March: yes, but more should be done.
Menchions: yes.
Mercer: Newfoundlanders should resort to more drastic measures. I feel they are not paying enough heed to the far-reaching reality of the campaign.

10. Are your verses intended as commentary about the existing situation?

Bonnah: yes.
Butler: I wrote those verses to strengthen and support Newfoundlanders' stand in its defense, and for the enjoyment I get in knowing I have helped.
Casey: yes.
Doran: yes.
Goobie: commentary.
Hiscock: commentary, and I also hoped to arouse the interest of others . . . most people are much too placid about things that really concern them.
Lane: written for fun.
MacIsaac: they are a rallying cry to others; some good Newfoundland seal hunt songs are needed, also stories and plays.
March: commentary, but also as an attempt to interest others to participate in countering the protest.
Menchions: they are just expressions of the way I feel.
Mercer: if I feel strongly enough about a subject, I submit it for publication in the hopes it will do some good.
Sheardown: I had hoped to make people think about the seal hunt as a way of life and to point out to others that Newfoundland sealers were neither cruel or unfeeling men, but rather a breed of brave, hard-working and proud men.

11. Have you expressed your concern in any other way?

Most informants replied they had discussed the situation with family and friends. Mary MacIsaac also sent a letter to the editor of the Toronto Star, and Elizabeth Sheardown sent her poem to the CBC Morning Side (radio program) poetry contest.

I do not have questionnaire returns from the following people: Crosbie, Hemeon, MacEachern, O'Driscoll, Pitts, Sulley, Scammell, and Ayre, but, what information I do have is included in the text.

CHAPTER IV

SUMMARY AND CONCLUSIONS

The sealing controversy is not restricted to a single event. As we have seen, protesters and counter-protesters have been arguing over the same issues for more than a decade. The sealers themselves have been only slightly disturbed at the ice; instead, the focus of world ire has been directed at the citizens of St. Anthony, at Newfoundlanders, and occasionally, at Canadians in general.

The success of the anti-sealing campaign is credible testimony to the persuasive powers of rhetoric. The attack by Brian Davies, Greenpeace, and others gained momentum through these arguments: unregulated slaughter of pups by cruel methods, species' depletion, hunting to support a "trinket fur" industry, and limited and uncertain economic return for three weeks' effort. And by concentrating on a limited number of issues--cute "baby" seals and inhumane killing by sadistic hunters--the protesters created an indignant public in Europe and North America.

Several explanations are offered for the protesters' success in gaining public and financial support: (1) the remoteness of the hunt, and (2) the lack of contradictory information to challenge protesters' claims. "They have recognized that it is easy to get people steamed up about something which is undoubtedly unpleasant to see. And because people know nothing of the activity, it is easy to get them to donate literally millions of dollars to stop it. The donation does not directly affect the donners' way of life."[1]

Protesters seek to bring international pressure on the Canadian government to stop the hunt, or at least to impose a lengthy moratorium while further research on the harp seal is conducted. Some encourage a boycott on all seal fur products. The audience is external, although lip-service is paid to the Newfoundland public by Greenpeace, who placed the following full-page ad in the St. John's Evening Telegram (1978): "While we can both still hear and think, we would like to present our case to you--the people most directly involved in this issue--and invite you to speak to us."[2] Brian Davies claimed, "If we're successful in ending the ship hunt (for seals) it is not my intention to interfere with the landsmen's seal hunt,"[3] but most of his appeals failed to distinguish between the two activities. (The majority of protesters are silent or ignorant about this point and consequently counter-protesters do not make an issue of it.)

The counter-protest effort argues from a human perspective; "Save our Swilers" was the response to the "Save the Seals" campaign. Humble, hard-working, God-fearing family men are the champions of the Newfoundland argument, with emphasis on economic necessity and occupational hazard and hardship. Statistics detailing the actual number of men engaged in the seal fishery are almost irrelevant in the counter-protest view. The attack on the character and integrity of Newfoundlanders is interpreted as slanderous and equated with blasphemy, for justification of the hunt is based on tradition and divine sanction. While protesters dismiss such arguments as out-dated and ecologically irresponsible, Newfoundlanders continue to cite these reasons as their rationale for supporting the seal hunt.

Acceleration of news by the media, as well as selection and dissemination practices unquestionably contributed to the subsequent emergence of counter-protest expressions. Several verse-makers acknowledged that their work was an immediate and reactionary response to news broadcasts (Sheardown and Goobie), and others attributed their compositions to cumulative frustration and anger at what they believed to be misinformed and irresponsible reports (O'Driscoll and Ayre).

Ostensibly, the 'defense' was directed at critics abroad, but most counter-protesters used local and provincial media as expressive channels. Their messages functioned principally to promote solidarity as well as to recruit sympathetic support from that sector of the public who had remained passive and silent while the protest gained momentum.

As noted, the outstanding characteristic of counter-protest is the highly emotional, reactionary message and delivery. Persuasion is accomplished by the skillful manipulation of public sentiment and values; events and known "facts" are used as evidence to support a position. According to Gregory Gizelis, "People pay attention to persuasive appeals, if the arguments presented sound reasonable to them. And, in order for them to sound reasonable, they must be in accord with the listener's ideology, cosmology, and world view."[4]

The expressive forms of counter-protest provide an index to the beliefs and values held by a particular group. William Jansen explored this aspect in his essay, "The Esoteric-Exoteric Factor in Folklore."[5] He articulated three features which make a group particularly susceptible to these sometimes unifying, sometimes divisive factors: isolation (by age, religion, regionalism, and the like); possession of special knowledge which either is, or seems to be, peculiar; and/or, the regarding of one group by another to be awesome, favoured, or admirable. "The esoteric part of this factor, it would seem, frequently stems from the group sense of belonging and serves to defend and strengthen that sense . . . The exoteric aspect of the factor is, at least in part, a product of the same sense of belonging, for it may result from fear of mystification about, or resentment of the group to which one does not belong."[6]

Cultural chauvinism and xenophobia are reflected in defiant verses that argue that Newfoundlanders have a precarious economic position, and therefore do not deserve the malicious assault by wealthier, self-seeking individuals. Counter-protesters are suspicious of protesters they do not know. They are resentful of people who come from away to protest a situation they do not fully understand and who are not subject to reprisal or criticism for their activities.

Negative stereotyping is a common feature of protest and counter-protest. The out-group is portrayed as excessively abusive and malicious; the in-group is praised for its discipline, maintenance of traditional values and worthy conduct. ". . . Stereotypes, not unlike folk proverbs, represent a unique combination of insight, projection, rationalization, and out-and-out self-gratification."[7] The reliance on stereotypes by counter-protesters may be viewed as (1) a defensive coping strategy to relieve hostility and frustration; (2) "substitutes for observation":[8] or (3) "an abridgement of critical thinking" in an emotional context.[9] Because interaction between the two groups is limited, both the protesters and counter-protesters are at liberty to make unchallenged remarks about one another. The degree of emotionalism which surrounds the issue is reflected in spontaneous expressions of counter-protest; typically, name-calling took priority over reasoned debate.

"Songs of persuasion," function to "communicate a specific sense of reality or view of the world."[10] Vernacular language and references to specific events are testimony that counter-protesters were really addressing fellow Newfoundlanders who would not require any detailed explanation.

Certain cultural values are discernible in counter-protest expressions. The abortion issue is an outstanding example, and several verse-makers condemn protesters who plead for "baby" seals and neglect the plight of aborted human infants (Pitts, Minnie Haw-Haw, Casey and others). Newfoundlanders perceive the controversy as man versus animal, or man versus resources whereas environmentalists do not make such a distinction. Their concern is with preservation of a global ecosystem--with man, animal and plant life having inter-dependent roles.

Although the verse-makers come from divergent backgrounds, they express their sentiments about sealing and the protest in a patterned, predictable way. Letters, calls to radio programs, verses, and songs are all typically reflexive responses to provocation, and their common rhetorical strategy is emotionally-argued rationalization and defense.

Frequent tonal switching, or inter-changeability of counter-protest rhetoric, should be considered in the context in which it occurs. Composers of counter-protest verse may be stimulated to express their opinion during periods of heightened emotion but, in the process of writing, they may recognize the advantage of other rhetorical approaches. I believe this explains why celebratory/condemning verses move towards a sympathetic/ reproachful appeal before concluding with adamant statements of justification. In other words, counter-protest expressions typically defend, then attempt to rationalize, and ultimately confirm their position with defiant or aggressive assertions of right.

These verses and songs are not likely to circulate in oral tradition, or be performed by anyone other than their original composers because of their extremely personal expression. Several reasons for the failure of songs of this kind to endure have been offered: ". . . songs that were sung in anguish are likely to sound humiliating in time of security," and, "songs of protest also are usually spontaneous outbursts of resentment, composed without the careful artistry that is a requisite of songs that become traditional."[11]

Although counter-protest verses can be appreciated by Newfoundlanders, they are difficult to repeat and memorize because they do not employ traditional folksong patterns. Incorporation of names, references to specific events, and the repetition of familiar countering arguments contribute to their esoteric nature as well as to their temporal popularity.

This collection is an attempt to demonstrate how counter-protest is a distinctive theme, specific to a particular people, time and place. Counter-protest expressions are valuable cultural indices because they make explicit what formerly was implicit. Through formal, thematic and content analysis--such as has been attempted here--it is possible to identify cultural preferences for certain rhetorical strategies as well as expressive channels. Most importantly, counter-protest expressions illustrate how certain expressive behaviours are simultaneously "a body of knowledge, a mode of thought, or a kind of art."[12]

Fewer Newfoundlanders go to the ice each March, yet sealing retains a metaphorical importance. In former times, songs and stories about the hunts were records of triumphs and disasters, adventure and fellowship; contemporary expressions, however, are quite different. Whether or not any of the songs or verses in this collection are reprinted or performed in succeeding years is not a particularly valid criterion for interpreting their significance; as social historical documents, they contain information about the public mood of a particularly critical decade. Although the tone and style of individual expressions vary considerably, there is no confusion about the message: Newfoundlanders will not readily relinquish their traditions for reasons alien to their views or way of life.

APPENDIX I

CHRONOLOGICAL SUMMARY OF PROTEST EVENTS

The Ontario Humane Society, in the March, 1972 issue of their publication, Animals' Voice, printed a list of their activities on behalf of the seals. I have borrowed extensively from that source, and use the initials, "AV," to indicate direct quotation.

1955 (May 30) — Meeting in Halifax, Nova Scotia, to discuss killing methods used in the seal fishery, chaired by Myles Murray, President of the Nova Scotia S.P.C. 'The meeting was held in response to public concern regarding humane practices which were stimulated by Dr. H. Lillie, who had recently observed seal hunting and made a film; Department of Fisheries biologist, Dr. David Sargeant, stated he was not satisfied with killing methods and recommended needed improvements . . . Dr. H. D. Fisher commented, 'inhumane killing was not the rule, but he did agree cruelty did occur due to haste and rivalry.' (AV)

1960 — "Tragedy on the Whelping Ice" published in Canadian Audubon, V. 22, no. 2 (March-April), pp. 37-41.

1964 — Ontario Humane Society submitted proposed amendments to the Seal Protection Regulations issued by the Department of Fisheries. (AV)

Artek film--Radio Canada commissioned Artek films to shoot footage of the Magdalen Islands seal hunt. Andre Fleury, Producer, with Uwe Koenemann, Assistant Producer.

(April) — "Murder Island," article by Peter Lust (Montreal Star) reprinted in West German newspapers.

Radio Canada broadcasts Artek film in May.

(July) — Prime Minister Lester B. Pearson sent letter to Montreal Star editor, '. . . It is the government's intention to see, that this fishery which has provided an annual crop for more than a century continues to flourish and is conducted with efficiency and humanity.'[1]

Munich and Hamburg (West Germany) humane societies enter the protest through news releases.

1965 — Department of Fisheries issued a statement on March 16 noting the reduction of the harp seal population to levels below maximum sustainable yield. Arrangements made for official observers to be present in the Gulf of St. Lawrence for the 1966 hunt. (AV)

1966 — Observers from Canadian and Boston humane societies attended the hunt. Skulls of slaughtered animals were examined to determine whether they had been dead before skinning. While the majority were, a few were not. Most observers believed the animals were unconscious and felt no pain. (AV)

June — Ottawa meeting convened by Minister of Fisheries, the Hon. H. J. Robichaud. Humane society officials, ship owners, a representative of the Newfoundland Federation of Fishermen, and regional Fisheries Department officials were in attendance. Regulations for the 1967 hunt were announced, including several recommendations proposed by the Ontario Humane Society. Revisions included:

- All sealers, including landsmen, were required to be licensed.
- The gaff was prohibited as a killing instrument, and regulation club sizes were established.
- Low-calibre rifles were outlawed.
- No incision could be made until the seal was dead beyond doubt.
- Sealing activity was restricted to the hours of 6 A.M. to 6 P.M.
- Fisheries officers were empowered to suspend licenses of violators immediately. (AV)

Henri Stadt, a former Artek soundman, produced his own sealing film because he objected to the Artek version.

1967 Observers at the hunt reported the effectiveness of the new sealing regulations. (AV)

Brian Davies and the New Brunswick SPCA made a film, "The Seals of the Ice Pans."

Peter Lust's, The Last Seal Pup, is published.

1968 Official observers agreed the hunt was as humane as any slaughter house operation and probably as humane as regulation and enforcement could ensure. (AV)

The Standing Committee on Fisheries and Forestry conducted public meetings in April to investigate the sealing controversy. 'The Committee concluded that grossly misleading information had been purveyed to the general public in Canada and abroad. Irresponsibility had been shown by the producers of the Artek film (1964), and by the CBC for not inquiring into its accuracy before screening.' (AV)

Henri Stadt viewed Davies' film and remarked, 'I think the film stinks and I think the man who did that film not only sold himself but all of us in the country--purely and simply.'[2]

Brian Davies was questioned about his income and the role of the New Brunswick SPCA in the "Save the Seals" campaign. Davies remarked: 'I think it (sealing) brutalizes a man, it makes him something different perhaps to you and I when he goes out into this very beautiful area and proceeds to club x number of baby seals.'[3]

John Lundrigan replied, 'I submit, Mr. Chairman, that I have met thousands of these sealers and the fact that we have the witness here today is an example that they are very humane because nobody has taken any vendetta against the gentleman.'[4]

1969 (summer) Brian Davies breaks with the New Brunswick SPCA and organizes, "The International Fund for Animal Welfare."

(Oct. 15) The Department of Fisheries announced a ban on the killing of whitecoat pups in 1970. All types of aircraft were banned from sealing operations. (AV)

1970 Official observers expressed satisfaction about enforcement of new regulations. (AV)

1971 Protests in New York city at Air Canada and Canadian consulate offices. "European Committee for the Protection of Seals" offered to pay sealers to stay home.[5]

Brian Davies escorted a group of American youngsters to the Gulf hunt to dramatize the issue.[6]

Minister of Fisheries, Jack Davis, established a "Special Advisory Committee on Seals and Sealing."

1972 Brian Davies returned to observe sealing in the Gulf.

The Interim report of the Committee on Seals and Sealing recommended a phasing out of the Canadian and Norwegian seal hunt by 1974, followed by a minimum six-year moratorium on sealing.

1974 No Newfoundland ships go to the ice; Newfoundlanders signed aboard Halifax-based vessels. Protest continues through the media.

1975 Observation continued by a variety of interest groups. Protest waged principally through the media.

1976 (March) Brian Davies hired a crew of airline stewardesses to join him at St. Anthony to go to the ice.

Greenpeace threatened to spray the seal pups with green dye, then rescinded the plan after a public meeting in St. Anthony, stating: 'We respect your style of living and we don't want to interfere with your livelihood; . . . join with us in stopping the Norwegians so there will be more seals for you in the future.'[7]

Richard Cashin requested Greenpeace co-operation to join the battle for establishing a 200-mile limit for Canadian fishing vessels.

A small demonstration in front of Decker's Boarding House in St. Anthony was conducted by Newfoundlanders protesting the presence of Greenpeace volunteers. Placards read: 'Save the Fishermen'; 'We want more than your dye'; 'Great Place--Wrong Issue'; 'Sympathy is not Enough'; 'Red Dye for Russian Trawlers, Norwegian Ships'; etc.[8]

1977 (March) Brian Davies rented the entire Viking Motel (St. Anthony) for his core of press and actress Yvette Mimieux.

300 demonstrators picketed the motel and surrounded Davies' helicopters until RCMP officers demanded they remove themselves or be arrested.

Brigette Bardot appeared in Blanc Sablon at the Greenpeace base camp. Her photo was taken with a stuffed seal pup, which later became the topic of controversy when press releases suggested the pup was alive.

Greenpeace member, Paul Watson, hand-cuffed himself to the winches of the "Martin Karlsen."

1978 (January & Feb.) The Newfoundland government scheduled press conferences across North American and in several European cities to present the Newfoundland case for sealing.

Brian Davies and Ray Elliott appeared in Europe to denounce the hunt as cruel and barbarous.

(March) Progressive Rights Organization sponsored an old-time, "Sealers' Send-Off," in St. John's, and organized concerts, displays and literature to tell 'the other side' of the sealing story.

The Mummers Troupe toured Canadian cities with their play, "They Club Seals, Don't They?"

U.S. Congressmen witnessed the hunt with Greenpeace members from San Francisco, Oregon, and Vancouver branches.

Greenpeace President, Dr. Patrick Moore, was arrested on two charges: for loitering in a public place (a temporary Fisheries Department office), and for obstructing the hunt.

Environment Canada | Environnement Canada

Fisheries and Marine | Pêches et Mer

APPENDIX 2

P E R M I T

TO WHOM IT MAY CONCERN:

Pursuant to subsections 12(5) and 12(6) of the Seal Protection Regulations, permission is hereby granted to

Cynthia Lamson

208 Cartier

St. John's

Occupation: Graduate Student

to approach within one-half of a nautical mile of any area in which a seal hunt is being carried out, subject to the following terms and conditions.

1. This permit is valid from March 10 to March 15, 1978 , for the Front Area only.
2. Transportation to and from the area of the hunt shall be by means of helicopter ______ and the helicopter is permitted to land within one-half of a nautical mile of any seal on the ice and fly over seals on the ice at an altitude of less than 2,000 feet.
3. A Fishery Officer must be onboard all helicopter flights authorized by this permit.
4. This permit shall be produced for examination upon the request of an enforcement officer.
5. Persons covered by this permit shall not interfere with seals or the sealing operations.
6. Non-compliance with the terms and conditions of this permit shall immediately render it null and void.

Dated at St. Anthony this 9th day of March, 1978.

Countersigned by ______

for Minister of Fisheries, Canada.

NOTES

The abbreviation ET is used for the (St. John's) Evening Telegram.

Preface

1. Albrecht, 1972:5.
2. Jansen, 1965:43-51.

Chapter I

1. Hughes, 1978:3.
2. A chronological summary of events spanning the years 1955-1978 is provided in Appendix I to facilitate the understanding of the sealing controversy.
3. ET, 16 March 1976:1.
4. Ibid.
5. Decks Awash, April 1976:8.
6. Op. cit.:9.
7. ET, 17 February 1976:6.
8. ET, 15 March 1977:1.
9. Ottawa Citizen, 16 March 1977:7.
10. Canadian News Facts, 1977:1739.
11. ET, 13 March 1978:1.
12. Personal communication, James Jeffords, 9 March 1978.
13. Albrecht, 1972:3.
14. Albrecht, 1976:149.
15. Koenig, 1975:475.
16. CBC-TV interview between Pamela Sue Martin and John Baker, (CBC-TV), 23 March 1978.
17. Connolly, 1978.
18. Letter from Martin Hurley, 19 March 1978.
19. Watkins, SNOCAN SC138.
20. VOCM Radio Action Line, 27 February 1978.
21. Personal communication, Kenneth Goldstein, 17 March 1978.
22. Lewisporte Pilot, 15 March 1978:6.
23. "Facts About the Seal Harvest," 1978:2.
24. Decks Awash, February 1978:1.
25. Richard Cashin, ET, 2 April 1977:6.
26. Decks Awash, February 1978:39.
27. The Seal Hunt, 1977:18.
28. Decks Awash, February 1978:10.

29. ET, 3 March 1976:3.
30. Clerical Caller, 1978:5.
31. ET, 1 February 1977:6.
32. The Seal Hunt, p. 19.
33. Scott, 1975:223.
34. Op. cit.:227.
35. Op. cit.:34.
36. Creighton, 1961:180.
37. Decks Awash, February 1978:13.
38. William McKay, Interview, MUNFLA 78-151.
39. ET, 17 February 1976:6.
40. ET, 1 April 1978:6.
41. ET, 25 March 1977:6.
42. Scott, 1975:213.
43. CBC-TV News, 6 March 1978.
44. ET, 10 March 1978:4.
45. Decks Awash, February 1978:54.
46. Polaris News, 9 March 1978:6.
47. Op. cit.:5.
48. Facts About the Seal Harvest, 1978:3.
49. Clerical Caller, 1978:4.
50. ET, 1 April 1978:6.
51. Public Meeting, St. Anthony, 14 March 1977.
52. ET, 2 March 1978:1.
53. ET, 23 March 1978:6.
54. Clerical Caller, 1978:5.

Chapter II

1. ET, 25 February 1977:6.
2. Halifax Mail Star, 18 March 1977:u.p.
3. ET, 3 March 1976:2.
4. ET, 15 March 1977:2.
5. ET, 30 April 1977:6.
6. ET, 18 February 1977:6.
7. ET, 3 February 1976:6.
8. ET, 23 March 1977:1.
9. ET, 15 March 1977:1.
10. Horwood, 1960:37.
11. Lust, 1967:44-45.

12. Kitchener-Waterloo (Ontario) Record, 12 January 1978:32.
13. Decks Awash, February 1978:34.
14. Op. cit.:5.
15. Weekend Magazine, 13 May 1978:8.
16. Decks Awash, February 1978:11.
17. Weekend Magazine, 13 May 1978:8.
18. CBC-TV, "Here and Now," 23 February 1978.
19. Personal interview, Ray Elliott, 28 February, 1978.
20. ET, 31 March 1976:2.
21. ET, 3 March 1977:6.
22. ET, 17 March 1978:6.
23. ET, 22 March 1977:6.
24. ET, 6 March 1978:1.
25. ET, 26 February 1976:6.
26. Ottawa Citizen, 31 March 1977:6.
27. ET, 31 March 1977:6.
28. Decks Awash, June 1977:6.
29. ET, 11 February 1978:6.
30. Arewa and Dundes, 1964:7.
31. See Fishman, 1956:27-67.
32. Sanger, 1973:230.
33. CBC-TV, "Here and Now," 14 March 1977.
34. Decks Awash, June 1977:6.
35. Recitation, 13 November 1977. LSPU Hall, St. John's.
36. Newfoundland Herald, 14 April 1976:23.
37. Poole, 1978.
38. Personal letter, 1978.
39. Letter to the Mummer's Troupe, March 1977.
40. ET, 24 April 1978:6.
41. Personal letter, 1978.
42. Abrahams, 1969:145.
43. Cooper, 1932:17-18.
44. ET, 21 March 1977:6.
45. Ibid.
46. Newfoundland Herald, 14 April 1976:22.
47. Szwed, 1975:156.
48. ET, 11 February 1976:6.
49. ET, 19 February 1976:6.
50. ET, 15 March 1977:1.

Chapter III

1. Brown, 1972.
2. Special thanks are due to Larry Malourin who referred me to Tom Goobie and to Peter Narvaez for his mention of Pat Sulley.
3. The term 'folk entrepreneur' is occasionally attributed to song writers in this category. See R. Serge Denisoff, Sing a Song of Social Significance, 1972.
4. Personal letter, 5 April 1978.
5. ET, 23 March 1978:6.
6. Ibid.
7. Newfoundland TV Week, 11 May 1977:52.
8. Poem posted on wall in Mummer's Office, LSPU Hall, St. John's.
9. Letter to Mummers, February 1978.
10. Personal letter, 1 March 1978.
11. Polaris News, 9 March 1978:9.
12. Personal letter, 31 March 1978.
13. ET, 21 March 1977:6.
14. ET, 24 March 1971:6.
15. ET, 13 March 1976:6.
16. Personal letter, 3 March 1978.
17. ET, 19 March 1976:6.
18. CBC-TV, "here and Now," 5 March 1979.
19. Personal letter, March 1978.
20. Ibid.
21. Personal letter, April 1978.
22. Paris Match, 1 April 1977.
23. Port aux Basques Gulf News, 1 February 1978:15.
24. Newfoundland TV Herald, 14 April 1976:22.
25. Newfoundland TV Herald, 19 May 1976:27.
26. ET, 10 February 1979:6.
27. In 1914, sealers from the vessel "Newfoundland" were caught in a blizzard, and 78 men lost their lives.
28. Recitation, LSPU Hall, 13 November 1977.
29. Personal letter, 10 April 1978.
30. Personal letter, 10 April 1978.
31. Personal letter, 30 March 1978.
32. ET, 16 June 1978:6.
33. Personal letter, 10 March 1978.
34. Personal communication, 23 March 1978.
35. Samson, 1963:41.

36. O'Driscoll, St. John's Folk Arts Council, 2nd Annual Festival, 3 July 1978.
37. Collins in Daily News, 25 March 1976:4.
38. Daily News, 18 March 1977:4.
39. Daily News, 10 January 1978:4.
40. Daily News, 27 February 1978:4.
41. Daily News, 23 December 1977:1.
42. Decks Awash, June 1977:6.
43. Memorial University Gazette, June 1977:14.
44. Tape-recorded in Miller Ayre's office, St. John's, 26 February 1979.
45. Press release from Bannerman Park, St. John's, 21 February 1979.
46. Personal communication, 10 March 1978.

Chapter IV

1. Decks Awash, February 1978:37.
2. ET, 9 March 1978:18.
3. Timmins (Ontario) Daily Press, 1 December 1977:u.p.
4. Gizelis, 1974:91.
5. Jansen, 1965:43-51.
6. Op. cit.:46.
7. Fishman, 1956:54.
8. Op. cit.:32.
9. Op. cit.:34-35.
10. Denisoff, 1972:2-3.
11. Greenway in DeTurk, 1967:114.
12. Ben-Amos, 1972:5.

Appendix I

1. Peter Lust, The Last Seal Pup (Montreal: Harvest House, 1967), p. 58.
2. Canada, House of Commons. Standing Committee on Fisheries and Forestry. Proceedings, No. 14 (April 15, 1969) p. 363.
3. Op. cit.:425.
4. Ibid.
5. ET, 3 March 1971:1.
6. ET, 9 March 1971:6.
7. ET, 10 March 1976:1.
8. ET, 13 March 1976:3.

REFERENCES

ABRAHAMS, ROGER
1968 "A Rhetoric of Everyday Life: Traditional Conversational Genres." Southern Folklore Quarterly, 32:44-59.

ALBRECHT, STAN L.
1972 "Environmental Social Movements and Counter-Movements: An Overview and an Illustration." Journal of Voluntary Action Research, I(4):2-11.

ALBRECHT, STAN L.
1976 "Legacy of the Environmental Movement." Environment and Behavior, 8(2):147-168.

AREWA, E. OJO and ALAN DUNDES
1964 "Proverbs and the Ethnography of Speaking Folklore." American Anthropologist, 66(6, Pt. 2):70-85.

BEN-AMOS, DAN
1972 "Toward a Definition of Folklore in Context." In A. Paredes and Richard Bauman (eds.), Towards New Perspectives in Folklore. Publications of the American Folklore Society Bibliographical and Special Series, XXIII. Austin and London, 3-15.

BROWN, CASSIE with HAROLD HORWOOD
1972 Death on the Ice. Toronto, Doubleday Canada Ltd.

CANADA, HOUSE OF COMMONS
1969 Standing Committee on Fisheries and Forestry. Proceedings No. 14 (April 15).

CANADIAN NEWS FACTS
1977 Toronto, Marpep Publishing Ltd.

CONNOLLY, JOE
1978 On the Front edited by Ivan Jesperson. St. John's, Jesperson Printing Ltd.

COOPER, LANE
1932 The Rhetoric of Aristotle. New York, Appleton-Century-Crofts.

CREIGHTON, HELEN
1961 Maritime Folk Songs. Toronto, McGraw-Hill Ryerson, Ltd.

DENISOFF, R. SERGE
1972 Sing a Song of Social Significance. Bowling Green, University Press.

DETURK, DAVID A. and A. POULIN, Jr.
1967 The American Folk Scene: Dimensions of the Folksong Revival. New York, Dell Publishing Co.

FISHMAN, JOSHUA A.
1956 "An Examination of the Process and Function of Social Stereotyping." Journal of Social Psychology, 43:27-67.

GIZELIS, GREGORY
1974 Narrative Rhetorical Devices of Persuasion. Athens, National Centre of Social Research.

HAULIN' ROPE AND GAFF: SONGS AND POETRY IN THE HISTORY OF THE NEWFOUNDLAND SEAL FISHERY
1978 Shannon Ryan and Larry Small (Comp.). St. John's, Breakwater Books.

HORWOOD, HAROLD
1960 "Tragedy on the Whelping Ice." Canadian Audubon, 22(2):37-41.

HUGHES, TOM
1978 Speech prepared for press release kit, Newfoundland Provincial Government tour, January and February.

JANSEN, WILLIAM HUGH
1965 "The Esoteric-Exoteric Factor in Folklore." In Alan Dundes (ed.), The Study of Folklore. Englewood Cliffs, Prentice-Hall.

KOENIG, DANIEL J.
1975 "Additional Research on Environmental Activism." Environment and Behavior, 7:472-485.

LUST, PETER
1967 The Last Seal Pup. Montreal, Harvest House.

ONTARIO HUMANE SOCIETY
1972 Animals' Voice (March).

POOLE, C. F.
1978 "The Soul of a Newfoundlander." Newfoundland Historical Society (lecture), February 20.

SAMSON, SOLOMON
1963 A Glimpse of Newfoundland (as it was and is) in Poetry and Pictures edited by Dr. Robert Saunders. Poole, England, J. Looker.

SANGER, CHARLES CHESLEY W.
1973 "Technological and Spatial Adaptation in the Newfoundland Seal Fishery in the Nineteenth Century." MA Thesis, Memorial University.

SCOTT, JOHN R.
1975 "The Functions of Folklore in the Inter-Relationship of the Newfoundland Seal Fishery and the Home Communities of the Sealers." MA thesis, Memorial University.

SEAL HUNT
1977 Canadian department of Fisheries and Environment (FS 99-16/1977).

ST. JOHN'S JAYCEES
1978 Facts about the Seal Harvest (pamphlet).

SZWED, JOHN F.
1975 "Paul E. Hall: A Newfoundland Song-Maker and his Community of Song." In Henry Glassie, Edward D. Ives, and John F. Szwed (eds.), Folksongs and their Makers. Bowling Green, University Popular Press.

Periodicals and Newspapers

Clerical Caller, United Church of Canada, Newfoundland Conference, January -March (1978).

Kitchener-Waterloo (Ontario) Record. January 12, 1977.

Memorial University Gazette. June, 1977; July, 1978.

Newfoundland Herald TV Week. April 14, 1976; May 19, 1976; May 11, 1977; January 11, 1978.

Ottawa Citizen. March 31, 1977.

Paris Match. April 1, 1977.

Port-aux-Basque Gulf News. February 1, 1978

St. Anthony Polaris News. March 9, 1978.

St. John's Daily News. March 25, 1976; December 23, 1977; January 10, 1978; February 27, 1978.

St. John's Evening Telegram. March 24, 1971; February 3, 11, 17, 19, 26, 1976; March 13, 16, 19, 1976; February 18, 1977; March 3, 15, 16, 21, 22, 23, 25, 1977; April 6, 30, 1977; October 1, 1977; February 11, 1978; March 6, 9, 10, 13, 17, 23, 1978; April 1, 24, 1978; June 16, 1978; February 10, 1979.

Timmins (Ontario) Daily Press. December 1, 1977.

Weekend Magazine. March 9 and May 13, 1978.

Other Sources

Action Line, VOCM Radio (St. John's), February 23, 1978.

Here and Now, CBC-TV. March 14, 1977; March 6 and 23, 1978.

Hurley, Martin. Letter, March 19, 1978.

MacIsaac, Mary. Recitation. "Good Entertainment Festival," LSPU Hall, (St. John's), November 13, 1977.

McKay, William. Interviewed by Dianne McKay (April 21, 1978). MUNFLA 78-151.

O'Driscoll, Gary. St. John's Folk Arts Council, 2nd Annual Festival. July 3, 1978.

Penney, Mavis. Cassette Tape. Public Meeting, St. Anthony, March 14, 1977. Viking Motel and Curtis Collegiate High School Auditorium.

Watkins, Reg. "200 Mile Limit Blues." SNOCAN SC138, 1978.

INDEX

Let’s be honest

It really does make a difference

VOL pour LA SAUVER des PHOQUES
FLIGHT to SAVE the SEALS
GREENPEACE '78